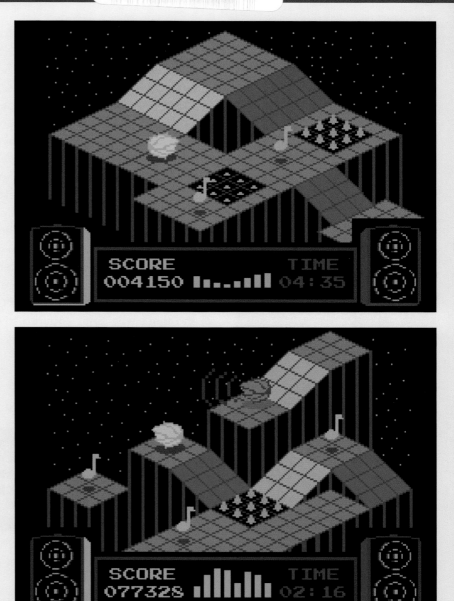

"...A MALEVOLENT RED CABBAGE THAT WOULD CHASE YOU THROUGH THE MAZES IN LATER LEVELS, EMITTING EERILY HUMAN SCREAMS."

03 GRIEF COPS

POLICE PROCEDURAL RPG WITH DEEPLY EMBEDDED THEMES OF LOSS AND EMOTIONAL DAMAGE.

YEAR
1981

GENRE
Police / RPG

DEVELOPER
Borksoft

FORMAT
Atari 2600, PC 286 4MHz, Coleco Telstar

In the heady days of the early 1980s, when home computing was expanding rapidly, most developers stuck to fun themes. Not so Borksoft, who quietly published an epic reflection on loss, disguised as a pulp police procedural, in 1981. To put *Grief Cops* into perspective, it's worth remembering that it's still used as a bereavement counselling tool by the UK's National Health Service. Let's be clear on this: those cops felt grief. Set in a Chicago precinct which had recently lost its beloved captain to a random shooting, the game followed the story of an officer trying to follow the letter of the law despite the trauma of losing his best friend. Taking the details of a speeding motorcyclist, a seemingly simple encounter, became a harrowing ordeal when you had to do it twenty times over during an increasingly distressing dream sequence. And that's if you got to the policing portion of the game at all: the main character could spend a full hour staring at the mirror while shaving, so play required patience to say the least. But while you could never quite get over playing *Grief Cops*, you could at least come to accept it, and that's why it has endured so well in the public memory.

At the time of going to press, Kelly Bork – the daughter of Borksoft's lead developer Keith Bork – has just released a sequel to her deceased father's game. Set 36 years after the original, it features the son of *Grief Cops'* protagonist, working to clear his dad's name from an ongoing corruption investigation as tiny administrative details threaten to emotionally unravel him. It's pretty heavy stuff.

VERDICT

Grief Cops could only charitably be described as 'fun' – nevertheless, its staggering emotional depth, not to mention its consistently sharp writing, was decades ahead of its time.

"THE MAIN CHARACTER CAN SPEND A FULL HOUR STARING AT THE MIRROR WHILE SHAVING, SO PLAY REQUIRES PATIENCE TO SAY THE LEAST."

04

JIMMY BUMSHOW

PUERILE EARLY PLATFORMER WHERE THE TITULAR CHARACTER MUST REPEATEDLY DISPLAY HIS BOTTOM IN PUBLIC WITHOUT ANYONE NOTICING.

YEAR
1981

GENRE
Toilet Humour / Platform

DEVELOPER
Boafus Home Entertainment

FORMAT
Philips Odyssey

Jimmy Bumshow, published by Boafus Home Entertainment in 1981, served as a stark warning of the dangers of reckless marketing. Following the release of Boafus' previous game, *Skeleton Fistfight*, the company ran a promotional draw giving one lucky player the chance to design their next game. The winner was a seven-year-old boy, and it really, really shows. *Jimmy Bumshow* featured a smirking wretch sauntering through a busy city, constantly trying to expose his behind. Every time Jimmy successfully revealed his arse without being caught, he gurned straight to camera and the game played a fart noise. Gameplay was limited to say the least, and parents were disgusted. Incredibly though, despite sparking a moral panic, the game was a raging commercial success, and briefly made the Philips Odyssey (for which it was the first third-party release) the clear leader in the second generation console market. Success was short-lived, however – a hurried sequel, *Poosaders*, starring Jimmy & his squire Billy Bumwee in a pathetic caper around C12th Damascus, was monstered by both critics and fans alike, and caused Boafus Home Entertainment to fold. Nevertheless, Jimmy's story isn't over yet – at the time of writing, it's rumoured the franchise rights have been bought by a major studio, with a release rumoured for 2019. May God help us all.

VERDICT

While it achieved astonishing luck with sales on initial release, history has recorded the near-unplayable *Jimmy Bumshow* as a staggering example of marketing gone wrong, and a prime example of the flood of shite that would bring the home console market to its knees in 1983.

"A SMIRKING WRETCH SAUNTERING THROUGH A BUSY CITY, CONSTANTLY TRYING TO EXPOSE HIS BEHIND."

05 CAPTURED BY THE SEX ORC

TEXT ADVENTURE THAT TURNS OUT TO BE ABOUT BEFRIENDING AN ORC WHO CAN'T ADMIT A FEAR OF INTIMACY DUE TO HIS NICKNAME.

YEAR
1982

GENRE
Fantasy Romance / Text Adventure

DEVELOPER
Lounge Wizards

FORMAT
Apple II, Atari 8–bit, PC 386 12MHz

Developers today rave about the potential for interactive storytelling to challenge how players see the world, and the indie scene is rife with subversions of genre, from Tired Seal's *Heartbreak on GunMoon 7*, to Rowdy Manner's *Call of Beauty*. It came as a surprise, therefore, for many to learn that this movement was already underway in 1982. *Captured By the Sex Orc* had been forgotten for decades, until Aimee Best stumbled across it in 2015. Best, who streams retro game playthroughs as AimzzBot, is celebrated for unearthing obscure and lewd games, then playing them through with a withering commentary. When she saw *CBTSO*, it looked like a classic of the form – the game's cover featured a badly painted orc, carrying a half-naked woman, surrounded by bare-chested barbarians, all drenched with oil and with abs like Toblerones wrapped in Parma ham. Indeed, the game's opening also followed the clueless misogyny playbook to the letter, with the protagonist – a princess – seized from her bedchamber and dragged to the Sex Orc's dungeon by musclebound goblins. The Sex Orc waggles his eyebrows and thrusts his pelvis in front of his troops, but once you are alone with him, he collapses into tears – it turns out he is terrified of sex, and has captured you in the hope of getting advice on changing his image. The rest of the game was understated, sober and utterly free of willies and boobs, with the real challenge being to decide whether to forgive the Sex Orc for his braggart past and help him achieve redemption, or to bring down his regime from the inside.

VERDICT

Captured was a fairly solid text adventure – but as a commentary on performative sexuality and fragile masculinity in high fantasy, it was inspired. Although it went nearly unnoticed in 1982's flood of home gaming releases, it has re-emerged as required playing for the 21st Century, and writer Marcia Kugelschreiber has been heralded as the postmodern genius she should have been recognised as at the time.

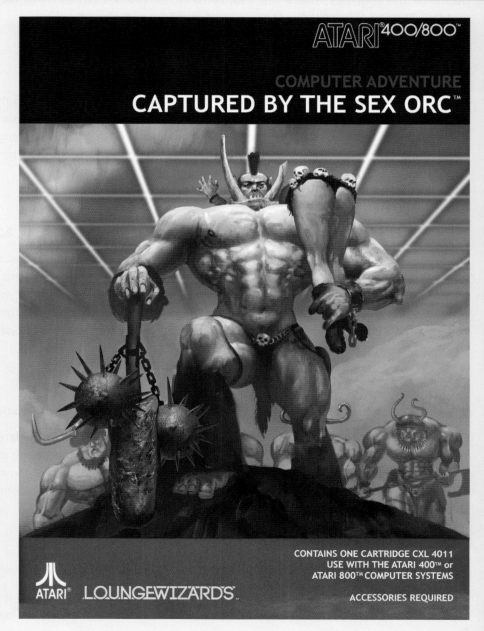

ATARI®400/800™

COMPUTER ADVENTURE
CAPTURED BY THE SEX ORC™

CONTAINS ONE CARTRIDGE CXL 4011
USE WITH THE ATARI 400™ or
ATARI 800™ COMPUTER SYSTEMS

ACCESSORIES REQUIRED

ATARI®   LOUNGEWIZARD'S™

"A BADLY PAINTED ORC, CARRYING A HALF-NAKED WOMAN, SURROUNDED BY BARE-CHESTED BARBARIANS, ALL DRENCHED WITH OIL AND WITH ABS LIKE TOBLERONES WRAPPED IN PARMA HAM."

5 SENSUAL ROMANCE GAMES

While *Captured By The Sex Orc* has won recent praise for subverting the largely sleazy 'romance' genre of the eighties, there are plenty of other games which have received critical acclaim through tackling the subject of love. Here are a few of our all-time favourites:

01 PANDA LOVE SERIES // Jollycom, 1992

Romance games have historically been written for the casual end of the RPG market, but the *Panda Love* series, from Japanese studio Jollycom, represents a notable exception. Just like panda breeding in real life, these games are *anything but casual* – *PL3*, for example, featured a DNA-matching minigame that only actual geneticists could comprehend, giving it a difficulty level spoken of in the same hushed tones of awe as the jetski level from *Combatfrogs*.

02 CONTAINER SHIP HIGH // Beast Mountain Games, 2007

In the storied history of the teen romance RPG, few games have achieved such breakout success as *Container Ship High*, the game that redefined the term 'commercial shipping.' *CSH* put the player in the shoes of a new student at a school for colossal freight vessels, and presented them with romantic dilemmas – for example, whether to date bad girl *Marie Mærsk* or prom queen *MV Barzan*. To make their choices, players had to rely not only on emotional intuition, but also the title's formidable in-game encyclopaedia of boats. As such, it was as much of a hit with ship buffs as it was with teens.

03 THE PYTHON PRINCES SAGA // Lucky Fruit Studios, 1990-Present

Despite its progenitor cartoon disappearing from American screens in the late 80s, the *Snake School* franchise became a cultural phenomenon in 1990s Japan, and remains popular to this day. One wildly successful spin-off from the property was the *Python Princes* series of snake-based dating games, launched on the Game Boy in 1990, which afforded diehard fans the chance to engineer charmingly innocent romances with beloved characters like Burma Bill & Reticulated Ronald.

04 HOLMES UNDER THE HAMMER // Chip Funbang, 2015

The increasing accessibility of games development in the 21st Century has led to a democratisation of games design, with titles too obscure (or risky) for studio release seeing the light of day thanks to individual dedication. One such game was *Holmes Under the Hammer*, an uncompromisingly graphic – and definitely NSFW – title created by someone who was really, really, *really* into the idea of Sherlock Holmes getting busy with comics hero Thor. The game admittedly had little to offer to people who *weren't* into that, but was hard not to salute for its dedication to a theme regardless.

05 WETHERSPOONS FETISH PARTY // Electric Tragedies, 2002

Unlike the other games in this selection, *Wetherspoons Fetish Party* could not in any way be described as romantic. Or indeed playable. It earns an honourable mention, however, for being the only adult–themed game ever to have been designed to be deliberately unarousing. Or so we hope. With extensive, grainy FMV sequences and endlessly awkward dialogue choices, this simulation of a kinky party in a budget UK chain pub played out like a searing recreation of an anxiety dream. Whatever you do, don't end up agreeing to the Lager Gimp's wager.

06 NOAH'S ROUGH MONTH

GUIDE NOAH THROUGH DIFFICULT AND OFTEN BLEAK CHOICES IN THIS APOCALYPTIC NARRATIVE MANAGEMENT GAME.

YEAR
1982

GENRE
Biblical / Management

DEVELOPER
Logic Brute

FORMAT
Commodore 64, Coleco Telstar, Atari 5200

Noah built the ark to last 40 days. It's now day 46, and the waters are yet to recede. Deck four is leaking. One of the cobras has bitten your son. You're down to the last barrel of meat for the tigers, and one of the unicorns is looking really ill. In short, things are looking grim – and this is only the first week of *Noah's Rough Month*. While the story of Noah has featured in plenty of Christian edutainment titles over the years, Logic Brute remains the only developer to have tackled the sheer scale of the logistical headache facing the Biblical hero. Tracking resources as diverse as lumber, tar, and hope, the game confronted the player with relentless management dilemmas, all of which could only be solved at the risk of sacrificing something precious and irreplaceable. It wasn't all doom and gloom – occasionally the game broke its text format for morale-raising minigames such as the Hippo Rodeo on day 64 – but overall, the tone was crushingly sombre. Once the doves ran out, and you were forced to send out eagles and hummingbirds in search of land, the despair really started to set in. Only the most determined players managed to keep things together until the flood subsided, and even then it was rare to make landfall with more than thirty or so species left in the hold.

VERDICT

Noah's Rough Month wasn't a pretty game, either graphically or in its grim scope, but the complexity of the simulation and its emergent dilemmas made it endlessly replayable.

"YOU'RE DOWN TO THE LAST BARREL OF MEAT FOR THE TIGERS, AND ONE OF THE UNICORNS IS LOOKING REALLY ILL."

MOTH EXPERT

PLAY AN ENTOMOLOGIST TASKED WITH CORRECTLY IDENTIFYING MOTHS BASED ON PHONE CALLS FROM THE PUBLIC, AND ENGAGING IN OCCASIONAL BOUTS OF SEVERE VIOLENCE.

YEAR
1983

GENRE
Moths / Edutainment / Action

DEVELOPER
Blood Vision Digital

FORMAT
Commodore 64, ZX Spectrum

After the flood of low-quality, rushed releases precipitating the crash in the US home console market in 1983 (See: *Hroop Blupper 2*, *BatPunch!*, *Billy Big Bollocks*), developers were desperate for new markets to release into. Luckily, this was also a time when games were first being seen as a potential vehicle for education, and so many studios rushed to stake their claim in the new genre of edutainment. Blood Vision Digital, a studio known for cranking out ultraviolent releases for the Atari 2600, showed particular chutzpah in remodelling a game for the edutainment market just three weeks prior to release. What started as *Lepidopterror*, a gruesome game about a hulking soldier tearing apart ravenous, man-sized moths, was released as *Moth Expert*, a simulation putting you in the shoes of a friendly entomologist. The aim of the game was simple: to take descriptions of moths from ordinary people, and match them to images from an internal library. Due to a falling out following layoffs, however, some of the original game's most shocking sequences were left in the game, as a hidden penalty for failing ten identifications in a row. Blood Vision tried to explain this away in their marketing ('the unusual dream sequences represent the moth expert's job stress!') but the damage was done: schoolchildren who discovered the hidden feature would fail the game's main task as hard as possible, turning it into an ichor-drenched celebration of ignorance which horrified schools. The game sank Blood Vision as soundly as any firm in the 1983 crash, but nobody could say they didn't make an effort.

VERDICT

Despite being a dreadful edutainment game layered onto the bones of a mediocre action romp, *Moth Expert* managed somehow to be greater than the sum of its parts – especially to bloodthirsty schoolkids.

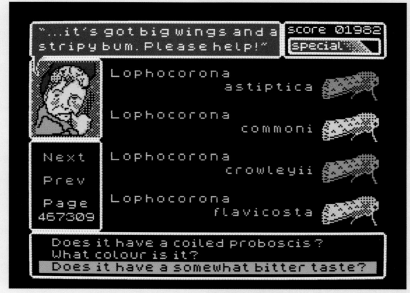

"THE UNUSUAL DREAM SEQUENCES REPRESENT THE MOTH EXPERT'S JOB STRESS!"

08 BEACHMASTER

ELEPHANT SEAL ACTION. SPEND THE WINTER BULKING UP ON SQUID, THEN TAKE TO THE SHORES AND BATTER RIVAL MALES TO CARVE OUT YOUR TERRITORY.

YEAR
1983

GENRE
Wildlife / Action

DEVELOPER
Tavuto Corporation

FORMAT
Arcade

Generally speaking, if you wanted to sell well in the arcade market of the early 80s, you went with space combat as a theme. Not so Jeff Bluster, the CEO of Tavuto Corporation, who after a near-death weekend of quaaludes and nature films decided that marine mammals were the *only* way forward. Enter *Beachmaster*, a rollicking powerhouse of a game featuring a 5-ton elephant seal and relentless, blubber–shuddering combat. Play alternated between fast-paced swimming segments, where the aim was to increase size by gulping down squid while dodging walruses, and frenetic breeding seasons involving savage duels with other gigantic seals. The thrill was visceral, with impacts accompanied by showers of blood and sand, and victories heralded by a deep synthesised voice pronouncing "Seal of Quality!" again and again. Such was the ecstasy of defeating the game's seventh boss, the Presidential Seal, that reports spread of players pushing over cabinets, honking, and gut–barging their friends into hospital. Such disturbances notwithstanding, the game dominated the North American arcade scene, and single-handedly fuelled a last hurrah for the golden age of cabinet gaming. Clones and sequels abounded, and even today it takes only the rasping bellow of an enraged seal to send many veteran gamers into a haze of nostalgia.

In 2007, to celebrate the release of *Marine Mammal Legends*, an anthology of Tavuto's arcade hits for the PlayStation 3, Beachmaster was given a graphical makeover and given a new bonus stage called Seal the Deal. This dramatic minigame saw players button-mash to build up their seal's rage levels, before bursting into a variety of rooms at the exact moments when history's most important deals were signed. The Magna Carta and the Treaty of Versailles were particularly unforgettable.

VERDICT

Although its bellicose celebration of primal violence wasn't for everyone, there's no denying that *Beachmaster* was both a technical triumph, and an inspired creative move at a time of near-stagnation in the arcade scene.

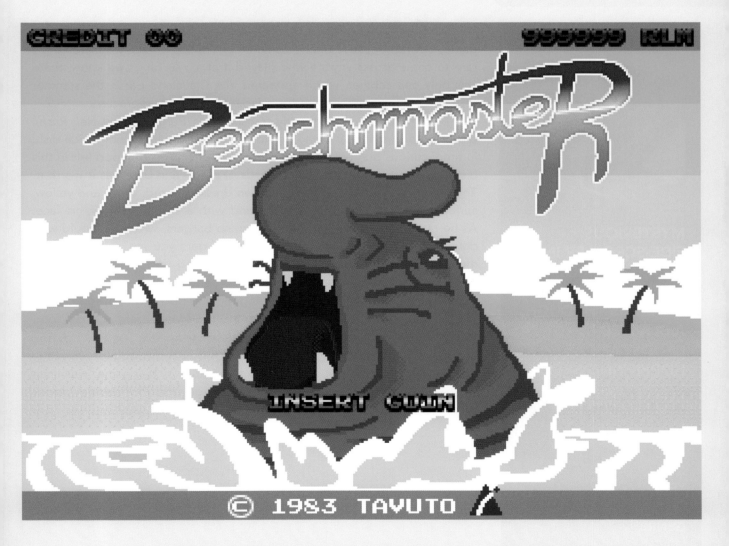

CREDIT 00   999999 RUN

BeachmasteR

INSERT COIN

© 1983 TAVUTO

"A 5-TON ELEPHANT SEAL AND RELENTLESS, BLUBBER-SHUDDERING COMBAT."

09

"THE CLOWN GAME"

MYSTERIOUS SIDE-SCROLLER IN WHICH A BURGER-LOVING JESTER CHARGES THROUGH A BLASTED LANDSCAPE AT HORRIFYING SPEED.

YEAR
1984

GENRE
Eldritch / Platform

DEVELOPER
???

FORMAT
Arcade

You can't talk about the arcade scene in the 1980s without mentioning this game, but not because of any commercial impact. In fact, it's increasingly rare to come across anyone who played it at all. As far as we know, there was only one cabinet, which appeared in a Cleveland bar in the summer of '84. It was unmarked save for a label bearing the characters バーガークラウンの地獄ラッシュ (roughly translated as *Burger Clown Hell Rush*), displayed only static, and had no slot for quarters – just a tiny metal dish. In time, curious punters discovered that for each drop of blood left in this dish, the game would offer 10 seconds of play – and boy, was it worth it. The game put you in control of a clown dressed in red, white and yellow, sprinting through a shattered wasteland with a savage grin on his face. As he ran, his arms would extend to grasp burgers, which he would wolf down without breaking pace. The more burgers you ate, the faster and more inhuman the clown became, until it ended up loping along on all fours leaving a trail of flames behind it. There is only one report of the game being completed, but the ending remains unknown – despite losing four pints of blood, the winning player elected to celebrate at a fast food restaurant rather than a hospital, where he soon expired. The next day, the cabinet was gone, and the bar appeared to have been closed for ten years. Even now, speculation abounds as to the nature of this game: was it an art project? Black-ops marketing? Or a message sent from another place? Whatever the case, we're glad it never came back.

VERDICT

Never again.

JUNE 19TH 1984

"FOR EACH DROP OF BLOOD LEFT IN THIS DISH, THE GAME WOULD OFFER 10 SECONDS OF PLAY."

10 WORM SALESMAN '84

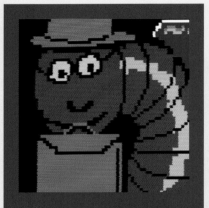

COMPLEX AND DILIGENT MANAGEMENT SIMULATION FEATURING A DEEP MODEL OF THE INTERNATIONAL WORM TRADE.

YEAR
1984

GENRE
Worms / Management

DEVELOPER
Lumbricus Developments

FORMAT
CompuGasm Konnect

With some 50 million players now registered to *Wormsell Online*, it's hard to believe the titanic *Worm Salesman* franchise began with this garage-programmed business simulation. Yet while *WS84* lacked the bells & whistles of subsequent entries, it had all the makings of a classic – the cultivation and upgrade of wormeries, the unlocking of new taxonomic branches, and the rich soil chemistry modelling all played human dopamine release systems like a piano. Indeed, to this day, the satisfaction of sitting back and waiting for a bumper crop of *Eisenia Hortensis* to mature for sale to Germany remains a hobby-defining experience to many gamers. *WS84* also broke major new ground for online gaming: with the game available as part of packages from online service provider CompuGasm, budding worm sellers could connect to a dynamic online marketplace shaped by the decisions of other players, and trade with strangers in real time. These days, it's hard to imagine a gaming landscape without *WS84*. Indeed, as the game's original tagline has it, 'The early bird may catch the worm, but he won't get a decent price for it without *WORM SALESMAN '84*!'

Later releases to the *WS* franchise would make online play a richer and richer experience – for example, the launch of *Annelid Analyst* in 1998 allowed players to assess and grade risk on portfolios uploaded by players of *Worm Salesman '97*, before selling them on to players of a third game, I*nvertebrate Investor*. In recent years, *Wormsell Online* has been criticised for 'pay to win' mechanics such as the purchase of new wormeries with real cash, but indications from this year's Lumbricon are that the game will soon return to its deep, earthy roots in subscription-based play.

VERDICT

Even if you despised both worms and business, it was almost impossible not to love *Worm Salesman '84*. A game it took an hour to learn, and a lifetime to master.

Worm Salesman '84 ™

Silkworm	China	450	− 3
Esenia Fetida	England	604	+ 1
G Gippsland	Germany	942	+ 18
	Arabia	027	− 11
	Germany	331	+ 2½
	England	420	− 3
	Arabia	004	− 244
	Austria	240	+ 2
	Japan	467	− 11
	Germany	045	+ 1
	France	420	− 3
	Poland	732	− 1
	China	511	+ 4
	Russia	123	+ 8
Longissimus	USA	099	+ 1

W0rmMstr01's Wormery

Next Trade
02:23:11

Wallet
$12,073

Activity
Wrmctchr1
Bought
GGlnd $921

Xwrmlrd16

"THE EARLY BIRD MAY CATCH THE WORM, BUT HE WON'T GET A DECENT PRICE FOR IT *WITHOUT WORM SALESMAN '84!*"

10 SERIOUS BUSINESS GAMES

Since *Worm Salesman '84* smashed onto the scene in the 1980s, there have been few game themes more popular than business. While space combat can be a laugh, and sport has its moments, there's surely no topic more thrilling than groups of people trying to make more money than other groups of people. Here are ten games that would like to add you to their professional network:

01 BUFFET LORDS // Strategovision, 2001

In this hex-based tactical combat game, it was your job to ensure a team of consultants monopolised the breakfast buffet on a hotel away day. Using special skills like Hungry Pete's Bean Inhalation Ray, it was a joy to make sure that not a morsel remained for potential competitors.

02 CONFERENCE NAPDODGE // Bunglesoft, 2016

A VR headset with a lead brick welded to the visor made *Conference Napdodge* a physical as well as a psychological challenge. Playing the role of a post-lunch businessman in the front row at a conference, you had to constantly battle through quicktime events to avoid nodding off to the game's 900 hours of genuine thought leadership footage.

03 EGGSECUTIVES // Pixelgits, 1995

In *Eggsecutives* you played a janitor, discreetly collecting the eggs laid by the board of a multinational corporation, then hatching them into tiny new businesspeople. Using a weird Lamarckian genetic model, the game allowed you to steer the skills of incubating professionals by feeding them different kinds of graphs and money.

04 MEETING KING // Searing Visionz, 2010

Bringing the noble art of meetings to the screen at last, this narrative strategy game won accolades for its punishingly realistic simulation of setting calendar invites, creating agendas, and annihilating the greatest number of person-hours possible in the process of deciding nothing. The game's first DLC pack, *AOB?*, was infamous for downloading the second you completed the main game, and taking twice as long to complete.

05 FTSE100 WARRIORS // Greased Wolf Entertainment, 1992

This ultra-detailed, side-scrolling beat-'em-up simulated fights between the CEOs of the companies with the 100 largest market capitalisation values on the London Stock Exchange at the time of release. An online play function linking power-ups to share values was mooted, but never implemented.

06 B2B JOURNALIST // TimeTrix, 2008

The first game to simulate the life of a trade magazine editor, this dismal RPG challenged players to appease software companies with reams of advertorial copy, all the while maintaining an illusion of integrity for the magazine's nineteen subscribers.

07 NETWORKER // Baffling Worlds, 1999

In this dark, business-themed point-and-click adventure, you played the role of a deceased salesman trapped in an eternal networking event between the worlds. Players could wander between expo stands for hours before twigging that they could only escape by piecing together clues found on the business cards of NPCs.

08 SUPER SACKER 3 // Dogsoft, 1987

A hit on the NES and then in arcades, this top-down management consulting action game saw players stride into an office, then hammer buttons to dish out rapid-fire sackings like bullets in a war. Power-ups allowed players to burst through office walls and begin sacking people, cars, dogs and abstract concepts on the street.

09 CHIMP TRADE ENTREPRENEUR // Gr8 Ape Games, 2004

A history sim harking back to the celebrated ape boom of 1926, *CTE* tasked players with managing Hootson & Screech, New York City's most extravagant chimp broker, as primate values skyrocketed and men got so wealthy their blood turned to champagne. The game abruptly veered into survival horror when one of the player's fellow brokers, blotto on victory, staggered through a reinforced window and released the firm's whole stock of chimps onto the trading floor.

10 BIG MIKE LUNCHTIME'S BUSINESS TRAINING '95 // Unknown, 2018

This web-based retro text adventure, written by a mysterious yet presumably handsome author whose name has been lost to history, saw players attempt to use a sales training CD-ROM from the mid-1990s, while unwittingly summoning the spirit of Big Mike Lunchtime, Revenant King of Deals.

11 THROUGH THE BUTCHER'S WINDOW

EERIE EDUTAINMENT GAME LINKED WITH A LOW BUDGET TV SHOW, CONFRONTING PLAYERS WITH MEAT-THEMED LITERACY AND NUMERACY PUZZLES.

YEAR
1985

GENRE
Meat / Edutainment

DEVELOPER
Carnival Funware

FORMAT
BBC Micro

As part of its computer literacy project in the mid-1980s, the BBC began producing simple, narrative puzzle games tying in with television series for the school market. After a string of wholesome hits such as *Pigeon Racers* and *Hyena Lass*, the broadcaster decided to let a third party studio get involved, and *Through The Butcher's Window* was allowed to happen. The series followed Dylan and Tiffany, two children who learn a Meat Spell from a red-faced wizard they find on a park bench. When they use the spell to try and steal sausages from a local butcher, they are sucked into the Flesh Dimension, where they must fight for their lives using strings of sausages as whips and bin lids as shields. It's tough viewing, and the game wasn't much more pleasant: one infamous puzzle involved calculating fractions as fast as possible to avoid Dylan sinking into a lake of giblets. Another saw players tasked with spelling words backwards to stop the Bone Ogre closing his jaws around Tiffany's hand. The game was unforgiving, disjointed, and deeply unsettling. In the end both series and game were pulled from circulation following complaints, but not before the game's code was reverse-engineered and distributed on floppy disks. Now anyone can play *TTBW* – and it's worth doing so, if only to witness how chilling an educational title can get.

> Smell the chicken, chant the chant / Find the courage in your heart / Throw the burger, shout – and Bingo! / Let's go through the Butcher's Window
>
> Sausage strings and bin lids clash / Solve the puzzles, win the cash / Hungry as a starving dingo / Deep within the Butcher's Window
>
> — Lyrics to *Through the Butcher's Window*

VERDICT

As a kid's puzzle game – especially removed from the context of its accompanying series – *Butcher's Window* was horrifying. Taken as an exercise in brutalist surrealism, however, it was strangely exquisite.

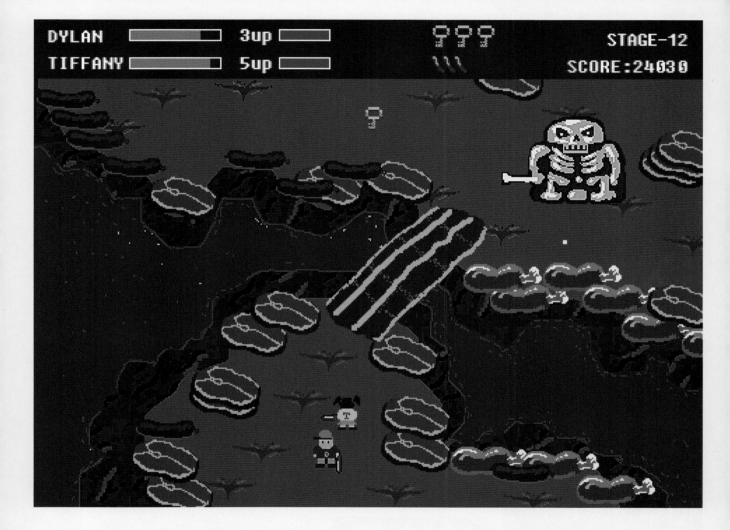

DYLAN ▢▢▢ 3up ▢▢▢ ♈♈♈ STAGE-12
TIFFANY ▢▢▢ 5up ▢▢▢ \\\ SCORE:24030

"...UNFORGIVING, DISJOINTED, AND DEEPLY UNSETTLING."

12 WORK KITCHEN ANECDOTE BASTARD

DIALOGUE-BASED GIT SIMULATOR IN WHICH THE PLAYER HOLDS COURT BY A KETTLE, LETTING CO-WORKERS ALMOST ESCAPE FROM ANECDOTES BEFORE REELING THEM RIGHT BACK.

YEAR
1985

GENRE
Reality / Simulation

DEVELOPER
Kingdoms of Astonishment

FORMAT
Commodore 64

Picture the scenario: you're mired in a meaningless office job, and have reached the point in the afternoon where you must go and make a coffee simply to give yourself an alternative to smacking your head repeatedly against the desk. When you arrive in the kitchen, with its mold-edged tiles and faint scent of bleach, he's there. That one guy. The one who never lets a conversation finish. He's microwaving soup. Getting near the kettle means passing his event horizon, but you're desperate and you take the plunge, knowing full well you are now bound to the spot by invisible bungee ropes of politeness. He asks you whether you're doing anything nice at the weekend. Fifteen minutes later, you're getting advice you don't want on choosing a shed. You're clinging to the door, edging backwards by the inch, but every time you try to close the conversation, he peels up another edge, grinning as he does it. It's like trying to hold down a squid. You can't do it, and he's fully aware of that. His soup's cold now, but he doesn't give a shit. This is sport to him. And *Work Kitchen Anecdote Bastard* is the game of that sport. Just *why* anyone would make a game of this is a mystery. And it's a mystery that may never be solved, as developer Kingdoms of Astonishment went bankrupt and disappeared one week after releasing it. It was their only game – and in the context of an incredibly specific purpose, it was perfect. It didn't even have an 'exit' option; the only way of making it stop was to unplug the computer. Bravo, Kingdoms.

VERDICT

This game was simultaneously perfect and abysmal. While its dialogue was perfectly observed and its simulation mechanics were flawless, the subject matter was so thunderingly banal that these attributes counted as negatives. Sadly, we may never see its like again.

"THE ONLY WAY OF MAKING IT STOP WAS TO UNPLUG THE COMPUTER."

13 DIRK BLUDGEON, WIZARD BAILIFF

URBAN FANTASY ADVENTURE; PLAY AS A POWERFUL SORCERER WORKING AS A LOCAL AUTHORITY BRUISER FOR A LAUGH.

YEAR
1986

GENRE
Debt Collection / Point-and-Click Adventure

DEVELOPER
BrutusArts

FORMAT
Apple IIe, Amiga 1000, NES

As advances in home computing brought about the rise of the point-and-click adventure game, most developers used the narrative freedom offered by the genre to tell stories of fantastic adventure. BrutusArts, by contrast (a studio that would later become known as masters of the format) made their debut with the surprisingly nihilistic *Dirk Bludgeon*. The protagonist, a being from another world with astonishing magical powers, had travelled to 1980s Bradford as a sort of grief tourist, to work as hired muscle for the local council. While he had the power to instantly fix the lives of the people he was collecting money from, at first the game only rewarded magical actions such as bashing down doors with feathers, and levitating tellies out of windows. The hardest thing about all this was how easy it was to accept as normal – indeed, the game was written so well that after a while, the player began to *relish* acting like Dirk. Even when the story did permit you to start acting compassionately to debtors, you were so hardened to Dirk's burly ways that you kept treating them as brutally as possible. At the game's end, when Dirk finally turned to the camera and winked before disappearing home, you realised you'd had the Stanford Prison Experiment done on you in an adventure game. While subsequent BrutusArts releases like *Viva Las Magus* and *Tragic Carpet* also played with the themes of wizards and moral ambiguity, it's quietly acknowledged that this sub-genre peaked in its first outing.

VERDICT

Despite being beset by long loading times and some needlessly obtuse puzzles, *Dirk Bludgeon's* gritty visuals and razor-sharp dialogue staked an early claim for BrutusArts as masters of adventure.

"AT FIRST THE GAME ONLY REWARDED MAGICAL ACTIONS SUCH AS BASHING DOWN DOORS WITH FEATHERS, AND LEVITATING TELLIES OUT OF WINDOWS."

14

JUDGE DREDD'S WINDY DAY

FACILE USE OF THE SF LICENSE WHERE ANVIL-JAWED LAWMAN DREDD IS REPEATEDLY THWARTED BY FLATULENCE ON A PLATFORM ADVENTURE.

YEAR
1986

GENRE
Sci-Fi / Guffs / Action

DEVELOPER
Foabus Home Entertainment

FORMAT
NES, Commodore 64

It was 1986, home gaming was finally on the mend after the 'Atari' crash of three years earlier, and British SF comic *2000 AD* was looking to get involved by licensing a game around their flagship character Judge Dredd. After a boozy meeting with developers Foabus Home Entertainment, *2000 AD*'s publishers felt their property was in safe hands – but they had made a dreddful mistake. As it turned out, the team at 'Foabus' were in fact the jokers behind failed software house Boafus Home Entertainment, using false moustaches and an anagram to disguise themselves. Boafus had produced *Jimmy Bumshow* (see p. 12), a game which had epitomised the puerile garbage that had sunk the market in '83, and now its creators had been given another crack at the whip. Working on code from an unmade *Bumshow* sequel, *Jimmy Bumshow and the Kingdom of Guff*, they slapped on some futuristic visuals and had *Judge Dredd's Windy Day* ready to ship in eight weeks. Commercial disaster seemed inevitable, but was miraculously averted – somehow, the game's combination of dystopian policing and fart lols was digital chrysopoeia, and turned what should have been utter shite into gaming gold. Players delighted in Dredd's discomfort as he stalked the streets of Mega-City One, stopping to chug a can of beans every few screens, and guffawed at the interposition of comedy fart noises in gunfights with perps. Indeed, the game's library of fart sounds was truly extraordinary, and players found themselves obsessively replaying levels so they could experience the full range of arsebarks, bumroars and trouser shouts on offer. Even now, Dredd's famous "Hurrrrrrngh" straining noise, followed by a wet hiss and the murmured word "justice," remains intrinsic to his character thanks to the legacy of this game.

VERDICT

Accidental as it may have been, *JDWD*'s combination of futuristic violence and toilet humour can only be described as sublime. You could point out any number of flaws in the game on an objective level, but all of them somehow served to make it more perfect.

"THE GAME'S COMBINATION OF DYSTOPIAN POLICING AND FART LOLS WAS DIGITAL CHRYSOPOEIA."

15 WRESTLECHESS

LIKE THE MONSTER CHESS GAME FROM *STAR WARS*, BUT ALL THE PIECES ARE CLASSIC 1980S WRESTLERS WHO BEAT THE PISS OUT OF EACH OTHER WHEN DECISIVE MOVES ARE MADE.

YEAR
1987

GENRE
Wrestling / Strategy / More Wrestling

DEVELOPER
The Number Mill

FORMAT
NES, Arcade

As a frantic obsession with pro-wrestling swept across the US in the late 1980s, and the NES brought about a new boom in console gaming, it was only a matter of time before the trends collided to create a supergame. The fact that chess somehow got swept up in the collision only made the end result more beautiful. In *Wrestlechess*, players controlled opposing stables of heels and faces, deployed on a simplified 6x6 chessboard styled as a wrestling ring. When pieces took each other, the perspective switched to side-on, and a bout of button-mash grappling took place. In a beautiful nod to the nature of pro-wrestling, these minigames could go on for some time, but only the 'winning' piece according to the rules of chess could actually win. *Wrestlechess* was beloved to gamers on this basis alone – but it prompted international hysterics when players discovered the Flip. The Flip was a button combo which, when activated correctly, caused the chessboard to be flipped, and the camera to zoom out to reveal the game WAS BEING PLAYED BY TWO WRESTLERS ALL ALONG. The players would then take control of these wrestlers and proceed to welly the shit out of each other, using the abandoned board – as well as bins, chairs and step ladders – to batter each other's colossal bodies. The revelation that *Wrestlechess* was a series of wrestling minigames nested inside a game of chess, *which was itself just a minigame nested inside a wrestling game*, was almost too much for some players to handle, and gave it instant legendary status.

VERDICT

Wrestlechess was not only a perfect encapsulation of how it felt to be a kid in the late 1980s, but a timeless formula for fun, thanks to its ability to turn from a strategy game into a brawl at the whim of human recklessness.

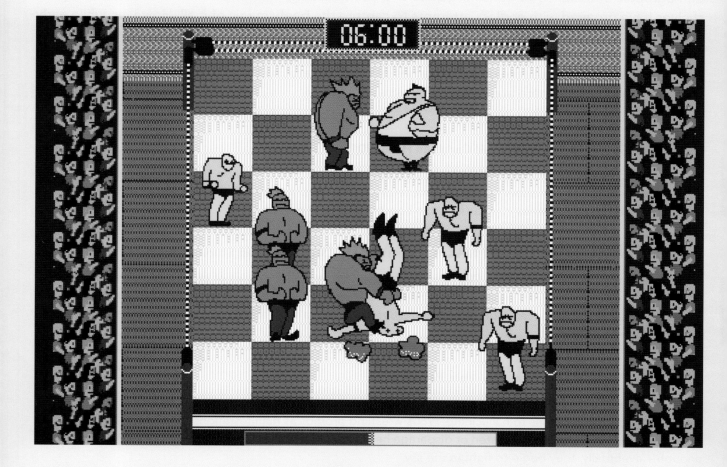

"A SERIES OF WRESTLING MINIGAMES NESTED INSIDE A GAME OF CHESS, *WHICH WAS ITSELF JUST A MINIGAME NESTED INSIDE A WRESTLING GAME.*"

10 POSTMODERN WRESTLING GAMES

The wild success of *Wrestlechess* only exacerbated the games industry's desire to feast on the demographic confluence of console games and pro-wrestling, and in the three decades since, the shelves have groaned with endless attempts to capture the beefy magic of it all. However, while early games took pro-wrestling at face value – as a deadly serious, competitive sport – later titles have come to appreciate it more for what it is: a baroque soap opera about the concept of gigantic men who hate each other. An entire genre of games has built up around the examination of wrestling as an abstract concept – and here are ten of the best:

01 WASSAILMANIA // Cerulean Hare, 2013

Taking as inspiration the old English tradition of Wassailing, where people sang to apple trees to make them try harder or something, this low key pagan masterpiece put the player in charge of a squad of wrestlers in an orchard, belting out showtunes in an attempt to boost agricultural output.

02 INTERCONTINENTAL CHAMPIONS // Big Lad Studios, 2017

In this ambitious narrative campaign, 20th Century history was retold as a series of pro-wrestling matches. World War One is a three hour royal rumble which achieves nothing, the Vietnam War pits a colossus in red, white and blue against a horde of smaller, more athletic wrestlers, and China's Great Leap Forward is a special move that damages its executor.

03 RUNNING WILD // Vole Patrol, 2011

A gorgeous and introspective story game, in which an ultramarathon runner suffering heatstroke in the latter stages of a desert run begins to hallucinate 1980s wrestling promos as manifestations of her inner turmoil. Some of the muscly spectres seek to threaten or disparage her, while others tell her she can do anything if she tries hard enough – eventually, they begin to fight in the sky.

04 PATHOGEN: W // Crepuscular Arts, 2007

FPS thriller in which a top-secret viral agent is released from a government lab, and the player must travel across infected territory to seek an anecdote. The game's big reveal is that the disease is Wrestlemania, and is causing the afflicted to wrestle uncontrollably with anything they see. A bit like *28 Days Later*, but with more people shouting "OH, YEAH!"

05 AUSTEN 3:16 // Default Moose Games, 2004

When a series of injuries forces legendary wrestler 'Stone Cold' Steve Austin to retire from the ring in 2003, he becomes trapped inside the works of Jane Austen, and can only escape by becoming the perfect gentleman. Things get interesting when Dwayne 'The Rock' Johnson appears as the local vicar, and the two men must put aside their feud.

06 TURKEYSLAM DESTINY // Nakamura Computer Fun, 2001

In this unsettling wrestling game from Japan, musclebound giants with roast turkeys for heads grapple blindly in a dim, greasy ring, occasionally stopping to ladle piping hot gravy over each other. While the game had a strong satirical context in its home market, it's fair to say this was lost in translation upon release in North America.

07 SLAMBASSADOR // Top Quality Entertainment, 2010

Burly fisticuffs & shrewd political dialogue abounds in this anime-styled treat for the Nintendo DS, where you play as the Wrestling Dimension's ambassador on earth. The game handled combat equally as well as branching dialogue, giving you very different solutions to the diplomatic problems presented throughout.

08 DEEP HORROR WRESTLING // The Meat Dungeon, 2015

A masterclass in Freud's concept of the uncanny, this supposed sports simulation was coded with a deliberately busted physics engine which made wrestlers occasionally crumple into jagged lumps, or merge with steel chairs and expand into a shaking mess of polygons.

09 STARSLAM // No Chill Developments, 2008

Space dogfighting game where instead of starfighters, the player piloted titanic clones of famous wrestlers, firing lasers from their mouths and bellowing catchphrases as they swooped majestically through the void.

10 WRESTLEMANIA: THE TEXT ADVENTURE // Keith Trouble, 2016

To the North is a GOLDBERG
To the East is a STEEL CHAIR
To the South is a SEA OF HUMANITY.

>_

16 SEAPUNCHER

PLATFORM SIDE-SCROLLER; STRIDE THE SEAFLOOR IN AN ANTIQUE DIVING SUIT, LAMPING FISH TO A SOUNDTRACK OF CRUNCHY 8-BIT SHANTY REMIXES.

YEAR
1987

GENRE
Nautical / Platform

DEVELOPER
Electryx LABS / Nintendo

FORMAT
NES

Thirty years after its release, *Seapuncher* remains emblematic in gaming culture as the title which ushered in a golden age of character-led platform games. At the time, however, it was far from a sure bet – when programmer Miyazawa Toyoshige suggested a mute, pugnacious diver as the main character for Electryx Labs' – a newly formed division of Nintendo – newest project in 1986, he was nearly laughed out of the door. Nintendo dominated the market by playing it safe, and wasn't keen on taking risks. Nevertheless, its president saw the potential in the character, and pushed ahead with development despite the protests of his board. When the game landed, audiences in Japan and the west alike fell in love with *Seapuncher*'s lush colour palette, its crisp sealife-biffing mechanics, and the squat, brassy form of its protagonist. *Seapuncher*'s quest was simple – to find and strangle the whale that punched his son – but it captured the hearts of millions. To trudge through a world of neon corals, smacking fish after fish while chiptune sea shanties belted out of the TV, was pleasure itself. Sure, there were concerns to be had over the game's message about man's interaction with nature, but sequels quickly made it clear that *Seapuncher* only punched *naughty* fish. Indeed, by *Seapuncher 4: Fist of the Fish*, the game's hero was working on behalf of marine wildlife to beat the smithereens out of evil oil company divers. And while he still hasn't said a word, *Seapuncher* remains beloved by fans, appearing in the form of a giant foam mascot at all of Nintendo's press events, and making avuncular cameos in many of their recent games. *Seapuncher*, we love you <3.

VERDICT

For many who grew up in the 1980s, *Seapuncher* epitomises 8-bit nostalgia. While it would later be superseded by rapid improvements in console technology, its visuals, sounds and character design have become timeless and iconic.

"TO TRUDGE THROUGH A WORLD OF NEON CORALS, SMACKING FISH AFTER FISH WHILE CHIPTUNE SEA SHANTIES BELTED OUT OF THE TV, WAS PLEASURE ITSELF."

17 BARRY THE SHRIEKING HORSE

LEVEL UPON LEVEL OF SERENE PLATFORM FUN, GROWING EVER MORE TENSE AS YOU AWAIT BARRY'S DEAFENING ARRIVAL.

YEAR
1988

GENRE
Animal Rights / Platform

DEVELOPER
Jolly Bludgeon

FORMAT
Sega Master System

In the rush of platform adventures that graced the console market at the back end of the 1980s, *Barry the Shrieking Horse* really stood out from the pack. You see, while most games were built around the identity of a likeable cartoon hero, *BTSH* was entirely constructed around the threat of an antagonist. And unlike villain-named arcade titles such as *Monkey Bigman* or *Bust-it Bill*, in which the boss was almost constantly on-screen and actively aggressive, you could go through most of *BTSH* without any hint of equine screaming. That was what made it so bloody unsettling. Playing as some forgettable idiot in green trousers, your task was to romp through colourful landscapes, picking up pleasant gifts and bopping lacklustre spiders on the head until they fell over. But then you would hear it: the brief, faint huffing of horse's breath. Sometimes it would come again, slightly louder. Sometimes it would go away entirely. But sometimes, just sometimes, the screen would smash-cut to an extreme close up of a horse's face in jarring, lurid colours, and play a deafening shriek through your speakers. Play would continue as usual afterwards, but the sense that nothing had changed – that nobody but you had experienced Barry – was fucking troubling. With no save states or pause function, it was a brave player indeed that managed to sit it out til the last level – a sprawling glue factory in which the game's pastel colours were swapped out for greys and rusty browns. As the game's bleak final task became apparent, so too did the nature of Barry's interventions – they were cries for help. Only the truly heartless completed this godawful game.

VERDICT

Nobody could say *BTSH* wasn't innovative in the way it handled the fourth wall, or its challenge to the unquestioning acceptance of platform heroes. But good grief, that final level. You can't unsee it. Not recommended.

"THE SCREEN WOULD SMASH-CUT TO AN EXTREME CLOSE UP OF A HORSE'S FACE IN JARRING, LURID COLOURS, AND PLAY A DEAFENING SHRIEK THROUGH YOUR SPEAKERS."

CURRY KNIGHTS

RAUCOUS CO-OP ARCADE ACTION FEATURING CHARACTERS LIKE SIR LAMB ROGAN JOSH AND BIRYANI THE MAGICIAN AS THEY SET OUT ON AN AROMATIC FANTASY ADVENTURE.

YEAR
1988

GENRE
Indian Food / Action

DEVELOPER
Mattbro Toys

FORMAT
Arcade

Based on the cartoon show of the same name, which was itself produced to market the line of action figures from toy giant Mattbro, *Curry Knights* is a rare example of a commercial tie-in that turned out to be an absolute banger of a game. It told the story of four warriors who, after banishing the evil Lord Chutney from their kingdom, are transformed into suits of armour full of enchanted curry and must embark on a quest to regain their human forms. The pace of play was blistering, the graphics were as rich and chunky as a high-end balti, and the audio was top-notch: as well as a soundtrack of medieval riffs and digitised sitars, the use of sampled speech was unheard of for its time. Indeed, the sound of King Jalfrezi threatening to ransack a dhansak, or Lord Chutney casting the spell Korma Trauma, remain familiar today thanks to endless sampling by EDM artists. Of course, the game wasn't perfect – at times the levels were samey, and the old trick of bringing back low-level enemies with a red paintjob and twice the hitpoints got old fast – but for what amounted to a toy advert, it was bloody marvellous.

Gadzooks! 'Tis the new range of CURRY KNIGHTS, only from Mattbro!

SEE as the super–strong Sir Lamb Rogan Josh launches poppadoms from his Balti Blaster!

MARVEL as Sir Chicken Tikka Masala makes his steed, the noble Pilau, transform into a full curry house that seats 80 covers!

WITNESS Biryani the Magician's magic, as you twist his waist to release a cloud of REAL curry powder!

SMELL the majestic scents of King Jalfrezi, with FIVE authentic curry smells available!

– TV advert for *Curry Knights*, 1988

VERDICT

Curry Knights wasn't breaking much new ground when it came to game design, but as an audiovisual spectacle – not to mention an appetite stimulant – it was an utter feast.

"THE PACE OF PLAY WAS BLISTERING, THE GRAPHICS WERE AS RICH AND CHUNKY AS A HIGH-END BALTI, AND THE AUDIO WAS TOP-NOTCH."

19 PTARMIGEDDON

SIDE SCROLLING BULLETSTORM ABOUT AN ELITE COMMANDO TRAPPED IN A PARALLEL UNIVERSE WHICH IS ABSOLUTELY RAMMED WITH PTARMIGANS.

YEAR
1989

GENRE
Birds / Sidescrolling Shooter

DEVELOPER
BirdBurst Interactive

FORMAT
Sega Mega Drive, Arcade

The ptarmigan, a type of grouse with white plumage, is a mid-sized game bird found in tundras and highland regions worldwide. It is also, as console players discovered in 1989, a complete arsehole when it comes at you in 500-strong waves from 16 directions at once. They discovered this by playing *PTARMIGEDDON*, possibly the most bird-focused game released since *Maths Ostrich* dropped in 1985. The game put players in the shoes of the peerless Wayne Discipline, an American commando embedded with guerilla fighters during the latter days of the Soviet-Afghan war, who suffers from a terrible fear of birds. During an assault by Russian troops, Wayne gets angry and shouts, "I wish we had more army guns," a little too near an enchanted rug. "Oh-ho!" says the rug, during a rushed cutscene at the game's start. "Did somebody say MORE PTARMIGANS?" And the rest is history. Or, more accurately, the rest is 18 levels of ceaseless, squawking, feather-clogged action. It was classic bullet-hell gameplay – frenetic, and almost impossibly hard. But there's an elephant in the room when talking about *PTARMIGEDDON*. Much as it hurts to say it, it would've been better off without all the bloody ptarmigans. There was simply no variety to the game beyond shooting wave after wave of birds. Some were larger than others, and some fired pellets at you, but at the end of the day, every single enemy was a ptarmigan. It seems the game's developers were willing to go all the way for their title pun, even if it meant sacrificing the player experience. And while it's hard see the business sense in that, it's also damned hard not to respect it.

VERDICT

What *PTARMIGEDDON* loses in judgement as a gaming experience, it gains as a labour of love. It was only when you reached level 9 (Ptarmigan Plains Part 3) that you realised just how far this game was prepared to go in service to a single joke.

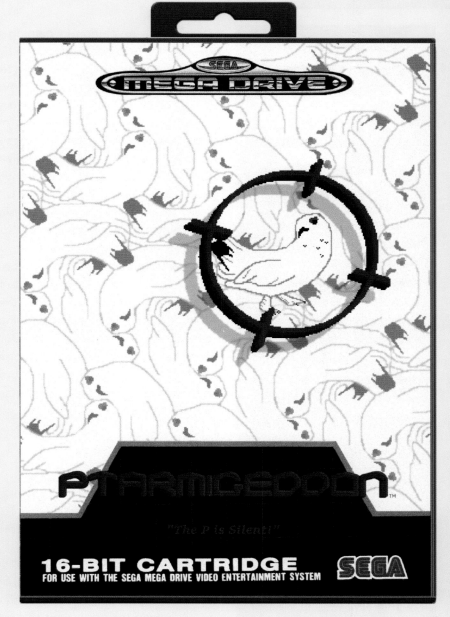

"DID SOMEBODY SAY MORE PTARMIGANS?"

20 STAR TREK: BEE ON THE BRIDGE

TENSE FMV GAME WHERE YOU PLAY AS JEAN-LUC PICARD, AND MUST STOP THE ENTERPRISE BRIDGE CREW TOTALLY LOSING THE PLOT BECAUSE A BEE HAS GOTTEN INTO THE SPACESHIP.

YEAR
1989

GENRE
Sci–Fi / Interactive Movie

DEVELOPER
Monochrome Mondays

FORMAT
Amiga 500, PC 386DX 20MHz

Despite the revolution in gaming technology taking place at the end of the 1980s, developers still found themselves struggling to meet consumer demand for more complex storytelling with the tools available to them. Enter the Full Motion Video (FMV) game – in which pre-recorded video was used to display action – and the seminal title *Star Trek: Bee on the Bridge*. In this tense 'interactive movie' based on the hit series, players were tasked with mustering Captain Picard's considerable leadership skills to stop his crew going completely mental due to a bee. Not some sort of tachyon–stinged space bee or anything – just a normal bee. But the crew really don't like it. Data's barks of alarm whenever it goes near him are really stressing Riker out, and Wesley Crusher's panicked flailing constantly threatens to set off dangerous space technology. It's Picard's toughest foe yet, and if he can't maintain order, it's only a matter of time before someone opens a window to shoo it out, dooming everyone to a spacey death. It was surprisingly spicy stuff. Yet while *ST:BotB* made clever use of footage from the show, it wore thin at times – in particular, play suffered from undue repetition of a clip where Worf lurched backward, panic in his eyes, from a superimposed dot. Dubbing was also patchy, with all of Riker's bee-specific lines apparently recorded under a duvet by a sibilant, gloating drunk. Nevertheless, the game's branching narrative and attention to detail won over fans and non-fans alike, and spawned a run of sequels that would long outlive the show itself.

VERDICT

While *Star Trek: TNG* itself managed to turn the exploration of space into something surprisingly pedestrian, *Bee on the Bridge* managed the opposite, using FMV technology to turn a stray insect into a crisis. The format was still rough around the edges, but as a proof of concept it really shone.

"PLAYERS WERE TASKED WITH MUSTERING CAPTAIN PICARD'S CONSIDERABLE LEADERSHIP SKILLS TO STOP HIS CREW GOING COMPLETELY MENTAL DUE TO A BEE."

A BRIEF HISTORY OF STAR TREK GAMES

The success of *Star Trek: Bee on the Bridge* essentially gave developer Monochrome Mondays a license to print money, and so the 1990s saw the Seattle-based developer absolutely monster the franchise for all it was worth. While there were a few gruesome missteps in the series (1994's *Dr Crusher and the Romulan Sex Festival* was particularly cringeworthy), they were by and large instant classics. Here are some of the unmissable entries in the series:

1990
STAR TREK: WHO SHAT IN THE TURBOLIFT?

This tale of scatological crisis dawns when Data finds a real honker of a poo in the *Enterprise*'s fancy lift, and gets incredibly upset. While it falls to Picard to find the culprit, the game later reveals him to be something of an unreliable narrator, and the player is led to the conclusion that it was the Captain's Log all along.

1992
STAR TREK: WHOSE TURN IS IT TO TAKE OUT THE BINS?

Taking out the bins is never easy in space, and things only get tougher when you have to remember the recycling rules across multiple interstellar jurisdictions. In this FMV stonker, the pressure of it all nearly tears the Enterprise apart. Riker spends half the game angrily brandishing the rota, Worf is shitfaced and having none of it, and Geordi La Forge keeps insisting it was his turn last week. In the end – and as ever – it's up to the long-suffering Picard to sort out the problem while his crew bickers.

1994
STAR TREK: Q'S BIG RECORDER RECITAL

Extradimensional trickster god Q has issued a capricious ultimatum: he will destroy the Earth, unless the *Enterprise*'s entire crew can learn to play the saxophone solo from "Baker Street" on the recorder in one week. Can Picard get their shit together? Can Worf handle his rage at the sound of it all? It's all pretty painful to listen to, but the set piece ending, including built-in recorder emulation for a PC keyboard, is spellbinding.

1996

DEEP SPACE NINE: WHO PUT THE EMPTY MILK BACK IN THE FUCKING FRIDGE?

As Monochrome's landmark series moved to the new setting of *TNG* followup series *Deep Space Nine*, so too did its tone step up to a darker and more mature level. In this installment, infamous for its unflinching portrayal of human rage, peace in the Alpha Quadrant is nearly torn asunder by a row that escalates over the discovery of an empty milk bottle in the titular space station's staff fridge. The game threw players an enormous curveball at its midpoint when, at the same moment as an alien warfleet emerges from a nearby wormhole, Captain Sisko discovers that someone has pinched the slice of ham he was saving for lunch, and completely snaps.

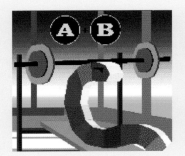

THE 90s

21

WINE
LORD

**PLAY AS A DOUR
ROBOT TRUDGING
ROUND A FUTURISTIC
SLUM, FORCING
CITIZENS TO CHUG
MERLOT. IF ANYONE
SOBERS UP, IT'S
GAME OVER.**

YEAR
1990

GENRE
Substance Issues /
Turn–Based Strategy

DEVELOPER
Goosepipes Software

FORMAT
PC 486SX 25MHz,
Amiga 500

"CITIZEN, HAVE YOU HAD YOUR WINE?" This phrase, intoned in a forbidding digitised tenor, became one of the most celebrated catchphrases of the early 1990s, thanks to this game. Produced by Glaswegian brothers Kenny and Jimmy Galbraith, working as Goosepipes Software, *Wine Lord* was a masterclass in dystopian cyberpunk aesthetics, and wowed audiences with its addictive tactical combat. Played from an isometric view, the game put players in the hulking iron shoes of W1n3-L07D, a law enforcement unit that looked like a cross between *Robocop*'s ED-209 and a man at the back of a horrendous pub, and wore a jaunty top hat. Using a support squad of hovering drones and net-wielding androids, players had to round up groggy citizens from hab units, parks and derelict buildings before feeding them cheap wine from a hose. Resistance came from teetotal rebel squads, using EMP grenades, tripwires and harpoons to fight back against the regime of enforced drunkenness imposed by BL0tt0, your AI overlord. While the Galbraiths had initially conceived of the game as a satirical commentary on alcohol marketing and government hypocrisy regarding substance control, it was received as a merry endorsement of getting pissed, which they accepted with wry silence. Although a sequel was proposed, funding problems meant it never came to light, and Goosepipes was disbanded in '92. Nevertheless, the Galbraiths remain in the industry, and are rumoured to be collaborating on a project about a prison for dogs, due in 2018.

"LOOKING A BIT STEADY ON YOUR FEET THERE, CITIZEN."
"PATRIOT, REPORT TO THE NOZZLE IMMEDIATELY."
"CHEER UP, CITIZEN – COME AND SHARE A DRINK WITH WINE LORD."
"COME ON, CITIZEN, IT'S JUST A LITTLE SOMETHING TO WET YOUR BEAK."
"WHAT'S THE MATTER, WATERBOY, AFRAID YOU MIGHT TASTE SOMETHING?"
– Digitised speech samples from *Wine Lord*

VERDICT

Although it's an incredibly depressing game when you stop to think about it, *Wine Lord* was a deep, engaging, and hugely replayable experience. The sound effects of rain – and sick – splattering on tarmac will stay with players for many years to come, as will the grinding entreaties of the Wine Lord itself.

WINE LORD

DEVELOPED BY
GOOSEPIPES SOFTWARE

"A LAW ENFORCEMENT UNIT THAT LOOKED LIKE A CROSS BETWEEN *ROBOCOP*'S ED-209 AND A MAN AT THE BACK OF A HORRENDOUS PUB."

22 RAGE BARON

INCREDIBLY PUNISHING RPG USING PIONEERING SENSOR TECHNOLOGY TO MAKE THE PLAYER CHARACTER STRONGER AS THE PLAYER GETS ANGRIER AND ANGRIER AT THE GAME.

YEAR
1990

GENRE
Uncontrollable Emotion / RPG

DEVELOPER
Irae Systems

FORMAT
Sega Game Gear

Ten years prior to *Rage Baron*'s launch, a humble game called *Cave Git* created a timeless archetype for RPG gaming: a dungeon crawl characterised by procedurally generated levels, random difficulty and permanent death for the player character. Despite being impossibly frustrating, games in this mould – Gitlikes, as they became known – were hugely addictive, and increased in popularity throughout the 1980s. *Rage Baron*, however, took things to a whole new level – in this brutal little number, progress could only be made by getting genuinely furious. The game's cartridge came with an adaptor, which connected to a blood pressure sensor cuff worn on the left arm during play. A resting heart rate and baseline pressure level conferred no change to the character's stats, but as stress became physiologically apparent, combat bonuses began to stack. And boy, did stress become apparent. If – or more accurately, *when* – you died in *Rage Baron*, the entire enemy contingent of the dungeon you died in would saunter on screen to gurn at the camera, show their arses, and clap sarcastically for a full, unskippable minute. They would be ushered onscreen by the Rage Baron himself, a bizarre character based on an old-timey fighter ace, who only ever appeared in the game to gloat at your death. On finally respawning, players with anything less than Shaolin-level control over their emotions would be fuming, and would be granted a little more power. To complete the game, however, one had to be worked up into a state of near apoplexy, and urban legend had it that a heart attack suffered during play would confer invincibility for the remainder of a run. While this was thankfully never tested, later examination of the game's code confirmed that, chillingly, this was indeed a feature. Since *Rage Baron* never resulted in a fatality, this can cautiously be regarded as a triumph of game design.

VERDICT

There's no other way of putting it: *Rage Baron* made players incredibly angry. But that, in the end, was its purpose. In the same way as you can admire a great white shark without wanting one in your home, it's hard not to respect the impact this game made on gamers, even at the cost of their physical and emotional health.

"THE ENTIRE ENEMY CONTINGENT OF THE DUNGEON YOU DIED IN WOULD SAUNTER ON SCREEN TO GURN AT THE CAMERA, SHOW THEIR ARSES, AND CLAP SARCASTICALLY FOR A FULL, UNSKIPPABLE MINUTE."

23 DRUID MECHANICS

CONTROL AN F1 PIT CREW OF DRUIDS AS THEY CAST ENCHANTMENTS ON CARS AND AUGMENT THEM WITH NIFTY HAIR AND BONE ACCOUTREMENTS.

YEAR
1991

GENRE
The Occult / Racing

DEVELOPER
The Venison Parallax

FORMAT
Arcade, Sega Mega Drive, Atari ST

With the release of Sega's 16-bit Mega Drive in 1990, developers had access to a platform with twice the power of the NES, and rushed to take advantage. Racing games were a boom area due to the speed of the new console's graphics, and a slew of rally and Formula 1 titles dropped in the decade's opening years. None were perhaps as creative as *Druid Mechanics*, which eschewed the high-octane thrills of the racetrack itself to focus on the mad scramble of the pit lane. The game told the story of a grove of 8th Century druids who had somehow travelled forwards in time for the sole purpose of winning the F1 world championship, using cars made from meteoric iron and beast hides, and driven by a pair of blinded warrior twins. Since the cars were completely shit compared with 20th Century efforts, it was up to the druids themselves to ensure victory by conducting elaborate pit lane rituals, anointing their cars with strange potions, and hexing competitors as they passed. The mixture of high speed rhythm-based button mashing and strategic play worked surprisingly well – trying to cast Magma Tyre on an incoming vehicle while directing a Fuel Golem to fuck up a competing crew, for example, was pleasingly hectic. And while the game's success was not enough to prompt an immediate slew of sequels, the franchise resurfaced in the late 2000s as *Carbarians*, an open-world epic set in a world where iron age tribes live alongside driverless, bestial cars.

Some power-ups from *Druid Mechanics*:

A rabbit's arse: Increases a car's speed, but gives the driver visions of primal terror.
Alligator scales: Doubles chassis durability, but makes the car prone to biting men.
Ash from a bonfire of moths: Permits brief periods of flight, but turns rain to magma.
A sprig of holly dipped in snake blood: Allows a car's driver to enter the Beast Realm.

VERDICT

Creative and thrilling, *Druid Mechanics* played like the monstrous offspring of the Monaco Grand Prix and a *Dungeons & Dragons* sourcebook – two great tastes that go surprisingly well together.

Enemy Car
passing in: 00:8

Alligator Scales

Next Pit Stop
updgrade in: 01:00

"THE MIXTURE OF HIGH SPEED RHYTHM-BASED BUTTON MASHING AND STRATEGIC PLAY WORKED SURPRISINGLY WELL."

RICKY FEATHERS / RICKY FEATHERS 2: JUST FOR HOOTS!

ERA-DEFINING PLATFORM FRANCHISE, FEATURING SKATEBOARDING OWL RICKY AND HIS STOIC CARER, DEREK.

YEAR
1991/1992

GENRE
Owls / Platform

DEVELOPER
Sega

FORMAT
Sega Mega Drive, Sega Master System, Sega Game Gear

While Sega had struck a blow to market leader Nintendo with the launch of the Mega Drive, they still lacked a mascot that could go toe to toe with the beloved *Seapuncher*. Enter Mark Best, the marketing prodigy behind Mattbro Toys' *Curry Knights* line (see p. 46), who Sega hired as head of marketing in North America with a view to creating a figurehead for the brand. Best came up with Ricky Feathers, a hyperactive skateboarding owl whose rebellious attitude, backwards baseball cap and wraparound shades were a perfect encapsulation of the youth zeitgeist in 1991. Ricky was a smash hit: where *Seapuncher* was stolid and lumbering, *Feathers* was dynamic, hurtling through landscapes in obsessive pursuit of the gold watches he craved, without a care in the world. It was a breath of fresh, owl-scented air. Indeed, when the scale of their success became apparent, Sega immediately began work on a sequel, *Ricky Feathers 2: Just for Hoots*. In *Hoots*, as it became known, Ricky was even faster and edgier, with a suite of new gimmicks to entertain players. Chief among these was his ability, after consuming enough watches, to emit a 'cyber pellet' that would expand into a television, into which he would leap to enter the three-dimensional 'mega zone.' *Hoots* also introduced 2-player functionality, with younger sisters and brothers able to take on the role of Derek, Ricky's hapless and exhausted carer, as he jogged anxiously after his charge. Of course, nothing in *Hoots* made any fucking sense, but it didn't matter – Best had struck marketing gold, and made an icon for Sega.

Near Misses – 6 proposed platform heroes Sega rejected before settling on Ricky:

Drill Sergeant: A hardboiled British WW1 officer with a gigantic drill for an arm.

Slugger: A Nordic giant punching vast carnivorous slugs in a dismal forest.

Anchor Man: A pain-wracked cyborg with an actual ship's anchor for a hand.

N0rm4n the C0nqu3r0r: A robot trapped in the Bayeux Tapestry with a hammer and a gun.

Turkey Boy: An optimistic boy with a roast turkey for a head, living in a dreamlike world.

Manvil: A police detective with the ability to suddenly and violently transform into an anvil.

VERDICT

If one game could be chosen as emblematic of the 1990s, it would be this. *Ricky Feathers* was the smash hit that fired the first shot in the console wars.

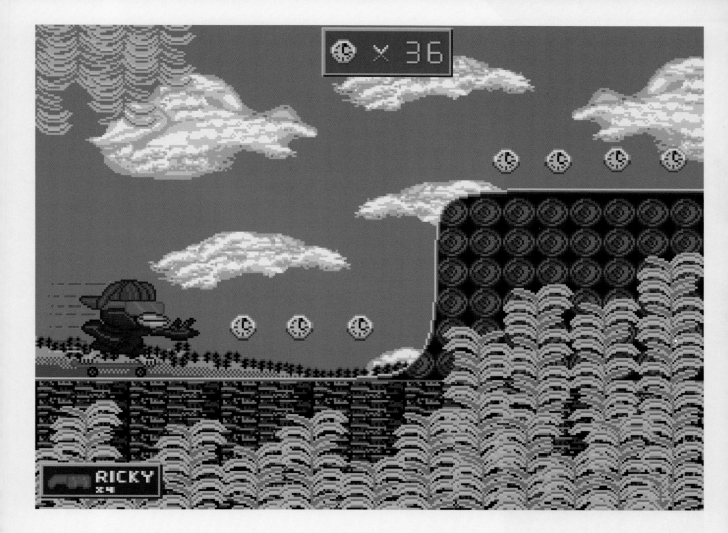

"A BREATH OF FRESH, OWL-SCENTED AIR."

25 BEASTENDERS

BRUTAL, GORE-STREAKED SCI-FI ACTION, BIZARRELY LICENSED ON POPULAR BRITISH SOAP OPERA *EASTENDERS*.

YEAR
1992

GENRE
Cockney Horror / Action

DEVELOPER
Digital Fist

FORMAT
Sega Mega Drive

Having stolen a march on its competitor with *Ricky Feathers*, Sega's next big play was to differentiate itself by offering games for more mature audiences, in contrast to Nintendo's more kid-focused output. Games like *Bastard Sword* and *Twilight of the Dogmen* were edgier and more gritty offerings than the market was used to, but the cornerstone of Sega's new 'bad boy' image was to be *Beastenders*. This blood-drenched rampage based on *Eastenders* – a UK soap about lovable cockneys – seemed doomed by its searingly broken combination of license and genre. In practice, however, it was fucking *art*. The low key British nihilism of *Eastenders* married perfectly with developer Digital Fist's bloodthirsty ambitions, and a gorgeous monster was conceived. *Beastenders'* premise was simple: when an alien carrier ship full of bioweapons crash-lands in the fictional London borough of Walford, it's up to local hardman Phil Mitchell to clean up the mess with nothing more than a claw hammer and a face like a cross thumb. The action is relentless, with Phil rampaging around Albert Square in a top-down orgy of blood, slime and digitised swearing. And when things get rough, Phil can summon his brother Grant, wielding a flicknife and a length of bicycle chain, to sort things out. But even then, *Beastenders* is a punishing game – the third boss (a scorpion with Dot Cotton's face) was notorious for stopping players in their tracks, and the level in which Phil descends to a sewer full of squidmen with liquid methane for blood was nigh-on impossible. Still, for fans of the soap and/or sci-fi horror in general, the game was a must-play, and remains beloved today.

VERDICT

Beastenders sparked full-on outrage in the press for its fountains of offal and outright glorification of pub fury, but even its most outspoken critics admitted it was a full-on treat to play.

"WHEN AN ALIEN CARRIER SHIP FULL OF BIOWEAPONS CRASH-LANDS IN THE FICTIONAL LONDON BOROUGH OF WALFORD, IT'S UP TO LOCAL HARDMAN PHIL MITCHELL TO CLEAN UP THE MESS."

10 LUVVERLY COCKNEY GAMES

Beastenders released something monstrous in the soul of the games industry. Countless frustrated creators, crippled for years by a fundamental inability to bring their ideas to life, suddenly found the means to express themselves via the theme of cockneys. Something about the mixture of urban quaintness and abyssal menace in the Cockney spirit really spoke to the interactive medium, and suddenly the theme was everywhere. Of course, every trend of this magnitude ends up going too far, and the craze for Cockney games has produced some dross over the years (*Crime Bloke* franchise, this means you). But it also spawned some gleaming gems, such as the following:

01 COCKNEY ORPHEUS // Shitegeist, 2017

VR retelling of the Greek classic, in which you attempt to walk out of a pub called Hades and into the overworld, followed by a pack of pearly kings. All the way through your cheeky anabasis you can hear their cheery songs – but if you so much as glance behind you, they are dragged back to the eternal knees-up of the damned, fancy hats and all.

02 BABS' BOONS // Hollow Dog Games, 1995

Hoping to strike the same licensing gold as *Beastenders*, this business sim put players in the shoes of *Eastenders* legend Barbara Windsor as she attempted to impose order on an out-of-control baboon breeding facility left to her by her deceased uncle. Truth be told, there was a lot of screeching and bums in this game.

03 GRAN'S TURISMO // Breadbin Home Disasters, 1999

Psychedelic racing game in which sports cars were swapped for hard-as-nails, chain-smoking Cockney grannies. Play centred around smashing buttons to swear viciously at other racers, while hurtling round the track at heartstopping speed in search of bargains.

04 TORTOISE HUSTLER 3: MURKY TERRITORY // Well Good Games, 2002

This spiritual precursor to 2009's *Wolfglance Tycoon* told the story of two glowering bastards in charge of a run-down exotic pet shop in Penge. Players were torn between aiding Gary, who secretly harboured dreams of breeding the world's hardest tortoise, and Neville, who just really loved organised crime.

05 CHAS & DAVE PRESENT: SPACE SAUSAGES // Thunderswan Interactive, 2005

Presenting the lighter side of Cockney living, this jubilant caper used motion-sensitive controller tech to let players throw sausages around in beautiful cosmic environments, while enjoying a soundtrack of raucous piano sing-alongs. Really good throws were rewarded with the sound of actual Londoners going proper bananas in a real pub.

06 GREASY SPOON HERO // Staggering Mammal Entertainment, 2009

While the hustle and bustle of short order cooking has proved fertile ground for many games in recent years (*ChipGod, Streetcorn, Chronicles of the Burger Lord*), few titles have matched the tension of *GSH*, where, as a lone cook in an East End café, it was up to you to assemble complex fry-ups for a torrent of hungry, barking villains.

07 DUCKSNACK: DESTINIES // Two Arbitrary Words Studios, 2014

In this surprise hit for the smartphone market, the player's task was to feed a morose duck crisps until it told them to fuck off in a thick London accent, deleting the app in the process. *D:D* was criticised for pay-to-win mechanics when an update allowed players to pay a quid to say "no, *you* fuck off" into the phone's microphone, and continue to feed the duck.

08 BEATS, BRUTES AND THIEVES // Pintglass Educational Software, 2003

Set in the underworld of London's clubland, this educational belter cast players as the fixer for a kingpin with a violent hatred of spelling and grammar mistakes. After carrying out your grim business in the side streets, the game's tensest moments came when you had to choose between different dialogue options in reporting back to the boss. One misplaced comma, and bang: you'd wake up dead in Leicester Square.

09 RAY WINSTONE'S BRUISER SAFARI // Digital Badmen, 2011

After an eccentric billionaire builds a wildlife park populated with clones of famous Cockney hardmen, disaster strikes when a hurricane knocks out the facility's power on its opening weekend. Electing to fight fire with fire, management summons Ray Winstone from his palace in space, and the race is on for him to batter the island's full quotient of villains before they can eat all the tourists.

10 WAR IN FACKIN 'EAVEN // Barenukkle Studios, 2015

This ambitious triple-A extravaganza pulled out all the stops with its Cockney retelling of John Milton's *Paradise Lost*. Set in an endless wasteland of derelict warehouses and 1960s tower blocks, it presented the tale of Lucifer's rebellion with a searing voice talent roster including Danny Dyer as the archangel Michael, Michael Caine as the father of creation, and Jason Statham as the shovel-chinned, beady-eyed Prince of Darkness himself.

26 PIG FALLING OUT OF A BIPLANE MUSIC VIDEO MAKER

COMBINE DISMAL HIP HOP BACKING TRACKS WITH PIXELATED FOOTAGE OF TUMBLING SWINE IN THIS PUNISHINGLY LIMITED MULTIMEDIA EXTRAVAGANZA.

YEAR
1992

GENRE
Falling Pigs / Music

DEVELOPER
Pixel Revelations

FORMAT
Sega Mega-CD, Sega Multi-Mega

With the advent of the compact disc, which could store hundreds of times more data than the cartridges used by existing consoles, developers were falling over themselves to take advantage of the new headroom available. The drive for quantity over quality led to some punishing initial failures, of which *Pig Falling Out of a Biplane Music Video Maker* was perhaps the most infamous. This game, so phenomenally shit it would become the subject of mass CD burnings, began with a workable premise: players would create music videos for their favourite songs, cutting together feeds of FMV footage in time with the music, then play them back and marvel at them. The problems came in the execution of the concept. In their rush to get the game together, and clueless as to the state of popular music, developers Pixel Revelations blew 90% of their budget signing BoatShow, an underwhelming hip hop duo from Nebraska, to provide music for the project. Meanwhile, the team assigned to acquiring video, on learning they had no budget left, fell into an abject panic. After a weekend of desperation, in which they filmed themselves getting hammered in a shed, they realised they still had no usable film, and resorted to begging for stock footage. In the end, all they acquired was a reel from a US Air Force experiment in the 1920s, in which pigs were dropped from biplanes to test parachutes. And so that's what they went with. The results were haunting: nothing said funky and fresh less than ghostly, sepia footage of pigs falling to their deaths, underscored with the mumbling lyrics and flatulent synths of BoatShow, and the game was universally despised.

How the world reacted to *Pig Falling Out of a Biplane Music Video Maker*:

"Is this meant to be an art project?" – *Electronic Pursuits Monthly*

"I'd rather eat my own hands than play this." – *Game Baron Magazine*

"Why can't I get these images out of my head?" – *Sega Aficionado Magazine*

"*Pig Falling out of a Biplane Music Video Maker* is inhuman." – *The UN*

VERDICT

As mathematician Ian Malcolm from *Jurassic Park* might have said, the developers of this game were so preoccupied with whether or not they *could* make it, they didn't stop to think if they *should*. Surely, this is a contender for worst game of all time – and for that reason, it's a classic.

"NOTHING SAID FUNKY AND FRESH LESS THAN GHOSTLY, SEPIA FOOTAGE OF PIGS FALLING TO THEIR DEATHS."

27

1950s BEACH BASTARD

SPRINT AROUND A BEACH, BOOTING APART WIMPS' SANDCASTLES AND GATHERING A HAREM IN THIS SURF ROCK-SCORED CELEBRATION OF VINTAGE BULLYING.

YEAR
1993

GENRE
Man's Inhumanity to Man / Action

DEVELOPER
Fat Snake Studios

FORMAT
Sega Mega Drive

There are few greater archetypes in Americana than the story told by the Charles Atlas pamphlet: after having sand kicked in his face at the beach, a wimpy man bulks up using the exercise routine of a benevolent strongman, then returns to batter his bully and win his girlfriend back from them. It's an age-old tale of underdog triumph, glistening with optimism, bootstraps attitude, and a deeply misogynistic view of women as property. As such, it was an astonishingly creative play for Fat Snake Studios, a developer known previously for introspective sporting titles like *Super Memories of my Father Baseball*, to make a game celebrating the role of the bully in the story. In *1950s Beach Bastard*, a top-down action game set on an endless beach during an endless American summer, your job was to maraud over the dunes, seeking out wimps and booting their sandcastles right into their chinless faces. With each adversary doused you acquired a girlfriend, which joined the train of consorts following behind you in a conga line of simpering obedience. The more girlfriends you acquired, the greater your physical mass became, until the game began to resemble 1983's *Beachmaster*. In time, previously defeated wimps began to return, rippling with bright orange muscle, for vengeance – and it was up to you to kick them into sodden, bloody splinters. The colours were oversaturated, the music was a grinding cacophony of 16-bit surf rock, and the social message was monolithically brutal. Nevertheless, the game near-perfectly encapsulated the essence of the primate dominance ritual, to an extent where even real victims of bullying found the glee of the hunt irresistible. *1950s Beach Bastard* was less a game than a wind, which stirred a dreadful sail in the heart of man.

VERDICT

In its own way, this game updated the Charles Atlas formula for the 1990s: rather than using chest expanders to gain the ability to beat the bullies at their own game, *1950s Beach Bastard* allowed downtrodden nerds to use technology to *become the bullies themselves*. Dark.

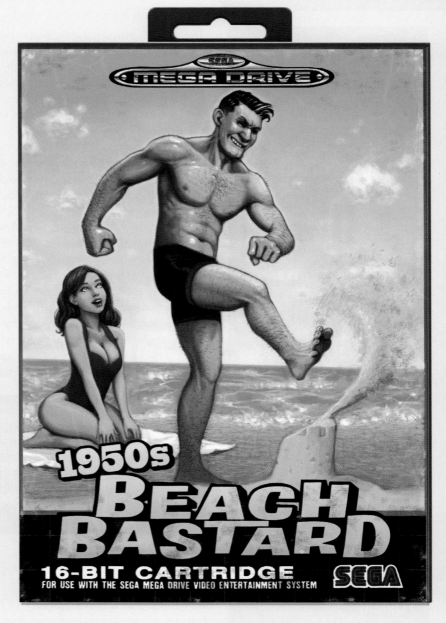

"YOUR JOB IS TO MARAUD OVER THE DUNES, SEEKING OUT WIMPS AND BOOTING THEIR SANDCASTLES RIGHT INTO THEIR CHINLESS FACES."

28 LEOPARD EXSANGUINATION TYCOON

BREED AND BLEED SIX DIFFERENT KINDS OF LEOPARDS TO ASSUAGE THE EVER-GROWING THIRST OF A LACONIC TYRANT IN THIS PIONEERING, IF ODDLY THEMED, REAL-TIME STRATEGY GAME.

YEAR
1993

GENRE
Birthdays / Real Time Strategy

DEVELOPER
Rednose Entertainment

FORMAT
PC 486DX2 66MHz

The scene: a dying earth, some time in a terrible future. The continents are blasted wastelands, the oceans are grey pans of silt, and the last cities teem with festering peasants. All labour, all art, all the dwindling resources of this enfeebled planet, are directed towards the perpetual celebration of a tyrant's birthday. Fields of withered crops are threshed for cake flour, while titanic grey mills grind confetti from the dregs of forests. And you, a hulking degenerate in the tattered raiment of a clown, are the chief party planner. This setting, which sat in stark contrast to the primary-coloured fun of other games at the time, was a *fucking strange place* for the real-time strategy genre to be born, but a fertile one nonetheless. While sequels would expand on the wider management of this birthday-themed dystopia, *LET* focused on the basics – constructing enormous mechanised farms to supply the Birthday Boy with his favourite tipple: leopard blood. All the while, players would have to fend off attacks from starving rebels, training units of despondent clowns and sending them to die on the barricades in order to keep the blood flowing. If that wasn't oppressive enough, occasional FMV briefings would bring you face to face with the despot himself, glowering, with party blower in hand, as he made cold inquiries on your progress. Play was harrowing, stressful, and incredibly difficult – most missions ended with the player character's execution for failing to meet quota, if the rebels didn't get them first. Nevertheless, the game was as engrossing as it was addictive, and tended to give players a new appreciation for the fragility of the Earth, the dangers of tyranny, and the importance of animal welfare.

"Good morning, commander. It will not have escaped your notice that today is, once again, my birthday. In recognition of this special occasion, the airborne ironclad *HMS Bouncy Castle* is to flatten the city of London in a jolly artillery barrage, and I will require refreshments during the show. As such, I ask that you secure 4,000 litres of clouded leopard blood before sunrise. You will also have your troops participate in nine rounds of Pass the Parcel. Do not fail."

– Briefing from *LET*'s third campaign mission.

VERDICT

As haunting as it was engaging, *LET* not only started an entire genre by itself, but prompted a quiet reassessment of man's place in a finite biosphere.

Sing the song, Commander

"MOST MISSIONS ENDED WITH THE PLAYER CHARACTER'S EXECUTION FOR FAILING TO MEET QUOTA, IF THE REBELS DIDN'T GET THEM FIRST."

29

BEHIND THE BINS AT BURNLEY CO-OP WARRIORS

BLEAKLY REALISTIC ARCADE ACTION ABOUNDS IN THIS SIDE-ON ONE-ON-ONE FIGHTING GAME SET IN A SODDEN NORTHERN ALLEYWAY.

YEAR
1994

GENRE
Post-Industrial Social Decay / One-on-One Fighter

DEVELOPER
Shattered Hand Studios

FORMAT
Arcade

Although the arcade scene of the early nineties was crowded with slick, colourful titles from Japan, it would be this game, forged in the dismal heart of England, that would become a worldwide hit, and establish many of the conventions for the one-on-one fighting genre. Elegantly dismissing the usual thematic fare of martial arts prodigies and international tournaments, the action in *Bins* centred around the alley behind a supermarket in a decaying Lancashire town, and the cast of hopeless bastards fighting it out to claim it as their own. With characters such as the Reeking Duke – a noble vagrant with a coat full of secrets and a face etched with regret – and Jimmy Needles, a creature of shadow and synthetic opioids, it was a refreshingly gritty take on an otherwise fantastical genre. The fighting too was shockingly consequence-heavy: while characters in games such as *Lord of Beatings* could walk away from fireballs intact, characters in this game got *injured*, staggering away from blows with dangling, shattered limbs, visibly dented skulls, and horribly slurred speech. *Bins*'s campaign mode was enthralling, with fights against playable characters interspersed with show-downs with bosses including the management of the Co-Op itself, a local bent copper, and Peter Pike, the MP for Burnley at the time of the game's release. But where it really shone was the versus mode where, as well as the familiar arcade cabinet controls, players had access to a massive foot pedal that would cause their character to hiss the most vile swear words known to the British vocabulary. While environments to fight in were limited to the alley itself, the cells of the local cop shop, and the garden of a closed-down pub, variety was introduced by weather effects including fog, rain, sleet, hail, drizzle, and football rioting.

Weapon power-ups from *Behind the Bins*:

Knackered golf club / Carrier bag with a kebab in it / An ill hound / Cricket ball on the end of a rope / Petrol station spanner set / An old claymore mine bought off a pub man / Nunchucks / Bundle of stolen cables / Enchanted broadsword

VERDICT

Bins wasn't pretty, and it certainly wasn't glamorous, but the visceral thrill of claiming the Bins after a twenty minute slugfest which left you with a busted ankle and an eye that only looks downward was impossible to match in any other fighter.

"A REFRESHINGLY GRITTY TAKE ON AN OTHERWISE FANTASTICAL GENRE."

30 EARTHWORM GYM

AS THE OWNER OF A RUN-DOWN ANNELID GYM, YOU'VE GOT SIX MONTHS TO GET THE LOCAL WORMS TOTALLY HENCH FOR THE WORM OLYMPICS.

YEAR
1994

GENRE
Invertebrates / Sports

DEVELOPER
Eggvision Interactive

FORMAT
Sega Mega-CD, SNES, PC 486DX4

Fourteen years after their hit debut *Look, Are You Coming In Or Not?*, developers Eggvision Interactive made their second indelible mark on the history of games with *Earthworm Gym*, a whimsical – if frustrating – take on the sports genre. Worms had been a popular theme for games since the foundation of the *Worm Salesman* franchise ten years earlier, but this was perhaps the first title to make players care about them as characters in their own right. The game followed ten of them – from the cowardly Terence Stretch to the aggressive yet feeble Pink Winston – as they attempted to get strong enough to enter the fabled Worm Olympics. As the proprietor of down-at-heel gym Wriggly Bruce's Muscle Barn, you (also a worm), had the job of bringing their dream to life. That meant a variety of button-tapping minigames, from skipping using another worm as a rope to weightlifting with acorns, as well as a broader metagame about managing the energy, nutrition and motivation of each worm. At the game's end, when you packed off your charges on the bus to Annelid City for the games themselves, it was always uncertain whether their adventure would end in triumph or defeat, as the action took place offscreen. But in a way, it didn't matter – over the months they had spent in your gym, you had found the champion inside each worm, and awarded them the gold medal of self-confidence. That was what really counted.

VERDICT

As a sports game, *Earthworm Gym* was nothing to write home about – its gameplay was monotonous and repetitive, and it lacked any sort of satisfying endgame. Nevertheless, the sense of nurturing and developing a set of scrawny underdogs into a team of confident sportsworms made it somehow far more enchanting than it had any right to be.

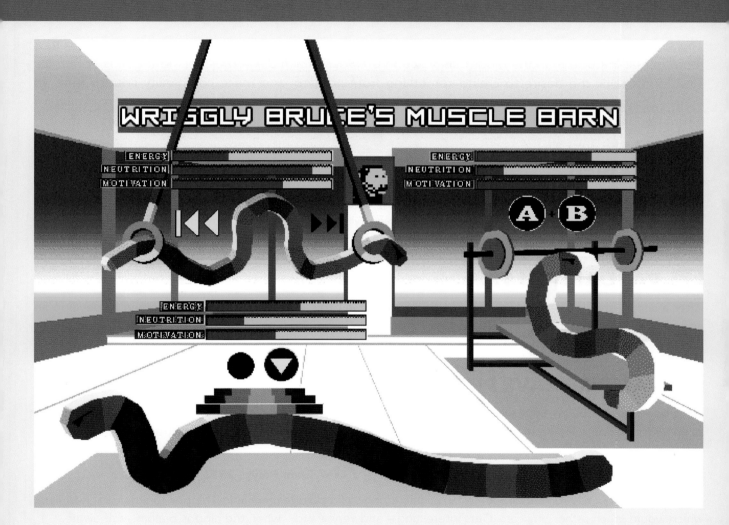

"OVER THE MONTHS THEY HAD SPENT IN YOUR GYM, YOU HAD FOUND THE CHAMPION INSIDE EACH WORM, AND AWARDED THEM THE GOLD MEDAL OF SELF-CONFIDENCE."

10 SERIOUSLY INTENSE MANAGEMENT GAMES

The simple satisfaction of managing an invertebrate fitness programme in *Earthworm Gym* spoke to a more gentle impulse than the bloodthirsty action of *1950s Beach Bastard* or *Behind the Bins at Burnley Co-Op Warriors*; the desire to create something from nothing, and make complexity flourish from an initially limited pool of resources. As gaming has grown more sophisticated, the management simulation genre has proliferated into a wide array of beautiful forms – here are some standout examples of the art:

01 SIM PIER // Lost Properties, 2001

Build, run and expand a pier in the golden age of the British seaside, then manage its decline in a bittersweet modern endgame. Expansion pack *The Grand Hotel* tasked players with managing a huge Victorian beachfront hotel, from its glory days as a holiday destination to its terminal years as a flaking husk where failed brass bands play for lonely racists.

02 RAT DAIRY 2147 // Broken Promise Studios, 2017

After a supply ship full of livestock embryos is destroyed in orbit, an early Mars colony is forced to develop an agricultural framework based entirely on rats. Featured an intriguing late-game built around trying to engineer rats to fill the ecological niches of all animals that are not rats.

03 VAMPIRE RAVE PROMOTER // Flying Ant Day Productions, 1998

Goth business simulation, where you must organise and market illicit blood raves, while staying one step ahead of an angry, sword-wielding man who wears sunglasses at night. Incredibly intense soundtrack.

04 ROBOT HIPPO DEALERSHIP '73 // Team Polyp, 2013

Manage a small family-run showroom in 1973 Hull, trying to flog crude mechanical hippos to a general populace which would much rather buy cars. Gets interesting – and very weird – when the hippos become self-aware.

05 ST MUNCHAUSEN'S // Big Old Toad, 1997

Almost unplayably dark hospital sim where the aim is to keep patients ill as long as possible without them realising it. Interestingly, the game's rights were eventually purchased by a US health insurer, and it quietly disappeared from the market.

06 GRIM BACKPACKER HOSTEL MANAGER '07
// Dirty Rotten Developments, 2007

Starting with a ramshackle bar in the middle of a rainforest, build dormitories and adventure sports activities to attract burnouts, gap year kids and sweating, testosterone-crazed liars until you've erased all hints of cultural authenticity in the surrounding area.

07 CHILI GARLIC SAUCE MATE? // Katabatic Labs, 2015

From the same studio that produced *Desolate Provincial Chinese Takeaway*, this unflinching simulation of running a kebab shop in South East London challenges players with managing not just the nightly business of selling death-meat to the profoundly pissed, but the emotionally complex life of the shop's proprietor.

08 CRAP ZOO ANGEL // Logic Brute, 1996

Perhaps in atonement for the bleakness they sowed in *Noah's Rough Month*, Logic Brute returned to the simulation of animal husbandry in this surprisingly uplifting management game. Starting with the kind of zoo where they feed the elephants chips and the bears look like they've seen war first-hand, it's your job to build an institution that educates, enlightens, and makes the world a better place.

09 DINOSAUR BUTCHER // Unforeseen Consequences, 2011

When a Yorkshire butcher with towering financial problems discovers a portal to the late Cretaceous behind some old beef in his store room, a whole new business opportunity presents itself. Gameplay revolves around hiring rough-and-tumble local lads to go on prehistoric meatpacking adventures, and paying the authorities not to notice the increasingly suspect bones appearing in your bins.

10 STYX ACCOUNTANT // Glandsoft, 2003

In Greco-Roman culture, coins would be left on the tongues of the dead to bribe Charon, the boatman who would carry their souls beyond the world of the living. In this weirdly straight-laced title, you play the dread ferryman's bookkeeper, tallying these bribes as well as noting purchases of new boating kit, in order to meet the tax requirements of the Kingdom of Hades.

31 POETIC JUSTICE

TURN-BASED COMBAT RPG: LEAD BYRON, KEATS, WORDSWORTH AND SHELLEY ON A NO-HOLDS-BARRED LYRICAL RAMPAGE THROUGH ENLIGHTENMENT EUROPE.

YEAR
1995

GENRE
C19th Literature / JRPG

DEVELOPER
Sublime Cataract
Developments

FORMAT
Sega Saturn

While the Sega Saturn enjoyed limited success, it would be wrong to consign its array of launch titles to history's bin along with it. *Poetic Justice* in particular, though it was admittedly a bit too weird to be a mainstream hit, was a veritable highbrow work of art. Just consider the premise: in the 23rd Century, Plato, Nietzsche and Descartes are reincarnated in the bodies of elite cyborg soldiers, dubbed the Killosophers, and sent back to the early 19th Century to utterly trash the Enlightenment. After witnessing the biomech ruffians ruin a village, Wordsworth phones his mates Keats, Byron and Shelley and urges them to tool up and fight back. Their crusade takes them across Europe, where they must defeat the minions of the Killosophers in turn-based duels, blending sword and gunplay with rhyme-based verse assembly. Of course, the Killosophers aren't their only foes — the poets are often their own worst enemies. Byron, for example, is an utter cock, and Keats can't stand him — halfway through the quest, they fall out spectacularly, and you must take the party to Sicily to seek mediation from Coleridge. Unfortunately, Coleridge himself is completely beasted on opium, and insists on a feud with Wordsworth. The game devolves into freestyle lyric bickering between the five men, which only ends when Nietzsche arrives in a nuclear-powered mech, forcing them to work together. Nevertheless, for a game full of so much egocentric cock-fencing, it has a commendable feminist final act — falling back from the blazing ruins of Vienna after Shelley's death, the poets seek aid from his widow Mary, who personally saves the Enlightenment with help from an army of Frankensteins.

> I wandered lonely as a cloud / That floats on high o'er vales and hills
> When all at once I saw a crowd / Of hardcore nutters, seeking kills
> Beside the lake, beneath the trees / Shooting blokes and snapping knees
> 'Twas time to call my hardest mates / And load them up with army guns
> We hollered then, to tell the fates / The mayhem we had just begun
>
> – Intro narration, *Poetic Justice*

VERDICT

If ever there was a franchise that deserves resurrection, it's *Poetic Justice*. While tactical combat RPGs have come a long way since, they've never surpassed *PJ* when it comes to theme.

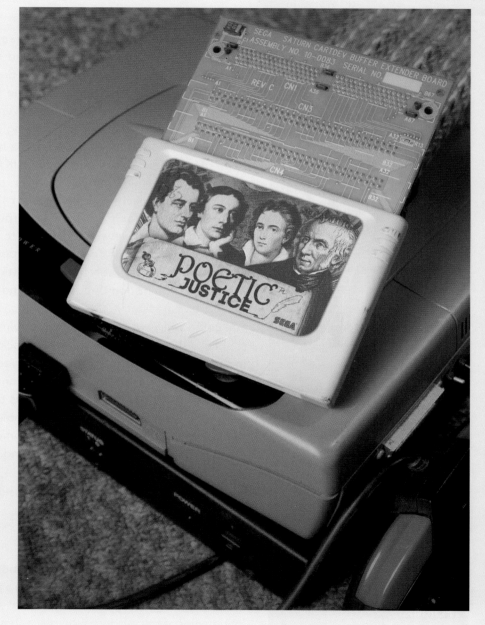

"TURN-BASED DUELS, BLENDING SWORD AND GUNPLAY WITH RHYME-BASED VERSE ASSEMBLY."

32 CALL CENTRE OF THE WILD

AFTER A CALL CENTRE IS BUILT ON THE SITE OF AN ANCIENT DRUIDIC HENGE, MAYHEM ENSUES WHEN ALL MANNER OF WILD BEASTS BEGIN SHOWING UP TO HIT THE PHONES.

YEAR
1995

GENRE
Beasts / Telesales / RPG

DEVELOPER
Big Mistake Software

FORMAT
Nintendo Game Boy

Following the success of 1989's *Wall Street Wolf*, in which a wolf inexplicably gets a job at a major stockbroker and must savage as many people as possible before being discovered, developers Big Mistake Software turned their eye to the handheld game market, and to a broader sphere of mistakenly-employed-animal misadventures. Released originally on the Game Boy, but with sequels still coming out today, this nifty little RPG put players in charge of an eagle, a wolf, a boar, a bison or a bear, which has been given a sales job in a sprawling UK call centre and sat amongst a sea of fragile, organ-filled humans. Thanks to an ancient curse, you appear to the humans as an acne-plagued youth called Nick, but the illusion fades as you maim more people, or if you underperform in a sales context. As such, the game's writing cleverly forces you to balance a meat-hungry approach to your colleagues with a genuine appetite for successful sales calls: get your claws out too freely without putting the requisite numbers on the board, and you'll soon be found out and hunted down by the call centre's ageing beastmaster. *Call Centre* is a casual game – it's the sort of thing you could whip out and play for twenty minutes on the way to work. But its simplicity shouldn't be mistaken for a lack of depth. While the wild-animals-in-the-workplace shtick is generally played for laughs, the game enters dark territory when it examines Nick's relationships outside of work. One of the easiest ways to advance in the game is to lure colleagues out to the pub, before mauling them on the cold cobbles at 2am – but in doing so, you risk becoming friends with them in the meantime. It's at that point that you begin to have some seriously concerning revelations about the reliability of the game's narrator.

VERDICT

As a game about wild animals going berserk in a sales environment, *Call Centre of the Wild* is a proper laugh. As a pitch-black metaphorical narrative about a young man whose homicidal tendencies are unlocked by the inhumanity of the modern workplace, however, it's a fucking masterpiece.

"BALANCE A MEAT-HUNGRY APPROACH TO YOUR COLLEAGUES WITH A GENUINE APPETITE FOR SUCCESSFUL SALES CALLS."

33 SEX HAVER 3

PROFOUNDLY ALIENATING SEX SIMULATION WITH AWFUL GRAPHICS, BASED ENTIRELY ON WHAT 9-YEAR-OLDS RECKON ADULTS GET UP TO.

YEAR
1996

GENRE
Doing Sex / Simulation

DEVELOPER
The Brothers Neal

FORMAT
PC Pentium 66

Massive advances in home computing in the mid-1990s revolutionised PC gaming, and led to a flourishing of first-person perspective 3D games. This in turn meant there were a ton of decent engines floating around, giving would-be games makers a huge leg up in producing their first playable efforts. One of these engines – the open-source build behind FPS *Angry Scottish Dad* – became the stuff of legend in the hands of Kenny and Liam Neal, a pair of precociously talented nine-year-olds with particularly fertile imaginations. The brothers Neal twisted *ASD*'s source code into *Sex Haver 3*, a bootleg monstrosity they distributed round local schools on a series of floppy discs, with the aim of making a small fortune and becoming playground heroes in the process. What they managed to produce was perhaps the most charmingly inept entry in the history of erotic art. Make no mistake, *Sex Haver 3* was hideous. But at the same time, it was so inaccurate it remains safe to play at work. The character models appeared to have been created with no reference to actual human anatomy, with guesswork genitals, and eyes that seemed to be murky windows into mankind's collective regret. 'Gameplay' was achieved via keyboard-controlled groping, and use of the mouse to click and drag body parts into position. The mouse wheel increased the tempo of pelvic thrusts, while synthesised voices moaned constantly, blurting out lines like "ooh, yeah," "do a sex on me," and "bung it in." The crowning glory of the game was that, in converting the code behind *Angry Scottish Dad*, the brothers hadn't quite figured out how to remove all the game's assets – merely how to conceal them. As such, in the game's second level (the Fancy Rolls Royce), a bout of gangly, wobbly intercourse is hard to get through without an irate, bearded face clipping through the car's door and roaring about the failure of the shipbuilding industry. For many critics and industry historians, that was the moment where games became an art form, and certainly where *Sex Haver 3* earned its place in the pantheon of all-time classics.

VERDICT

At once a damning indictment of British sex education in the 1990s, and a celebration of the entrepreneurial spirit, *Sex Haver 3* remains one of the most charmingly shit artefacts in games history.

"THE MOST CHARMINGLY INEPT ENTRY IN THE HISTORY OF EROTIC ART."

34 SPQR

SURVIVAL HORROR SET IN A ROPEY LOCAL MUSEUM, WHERE THE SHIT WAX ROMANS HAVE COME TO LIFE RAVENOUS FOR FLESH. *ALEA IACTA EST...*

YEAR
1996

GENRE
Romans / Survival Horror

DEVELOPER
Jolly Bludgeon

FORMAT
PC Pentium 75, PlayStation

We all remember the sequence. It's a rainy Sunday, in a town that hasn't turned out to be as fun as it looked on the brochure, at a museum that didn't even look fun on the brochure. You're on your own – but suddenly, the sense of solitude becomes profound; threatening, even. "When does this place close again?" you ask yourself, anxiously looking at your watch. It's 5.15pm. The museum closed at 5pm. Somewhere, the clank of a key in a lock echoes. Moments later, the lights go off. Panicking, you run to the exit by the gift shop, only to find steel shutters blocking your path. You're locked in for the night. You turn to assess your options, but something freezes you in mic-step. The waxwork Roman centurion that had stood by the gift shop entrance. The one with glossy orange skin and a faint, knowing smirk, despite eyes like slippery wax olives. It's gone. You put it down to poor memory and put it out of your head, rummaging in your pack to see what's left of your packed lunch. But then you hear it – the slow scrape of sandals on knackered floorboards, the clink of cheap reproduction armour in the dark. "Ave, citizen" intones a voice like graveyard clay, from too close behind you, and you run into the dark. So begins *SPQR*, the title which, even 20 years on, holds the gold standard for the survival horror genre. The graphics weren't spectacular, and the game played for a little less than two hours, but despite its modest production values, this simulation of being hunted through a provincial museum by wax Romans remains one of the most visceral experiences you can have behind a screen. It's almost impossible to play in the dark, especially with headphones, and the news that a VR remake is in the works means a whole new generation of gamers will get the chance to shit their collective pants at this masterpiece. As Decimus himself, the game's lumpen antagonist, would say, "I can't wait to tell you of the glory of Rome, citizen..."

VERDICT

SPQR is the reason a whole generation gets nervous in museums. While jump-scare horror is all the rage these days, developers could learn an awful lot from this masterclass in creating fear in games.

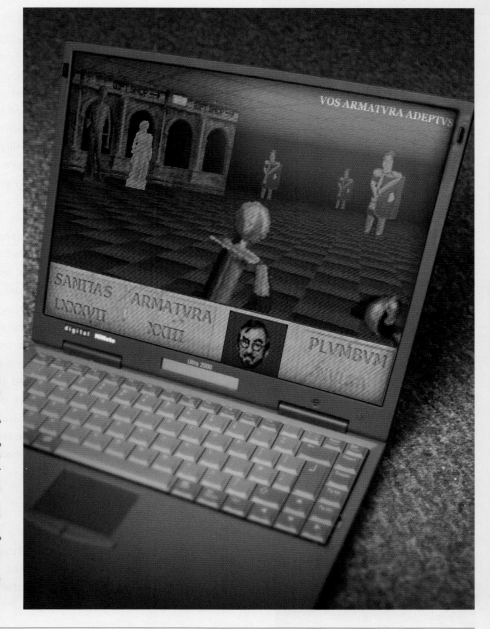

"THIS SIMULATION OF BEING HUNTED THROUGH A PROVINCIAL MUSEUM BY WAX ROMANS REMAINS ONE OF THE MOST VISCERAL EXPERIENCES YOU CAN HAVE BEHIND A SCREEN."

PETTY THIEF

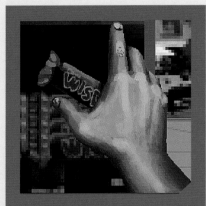

UK HIGH STREET STEALTH: ROB A WISPA FROM A NEWSAGENT WITH A BIT OF STRING, NICK A DOG LEAD FROM A POUND SHOP, STEAL PANTS FROM M&S.

YEAR
1997

GENRE
Minor Crime / Stealth

DEVELOPER
Broken Harpsichord

FORMAT
PC Pentium 120, PlayStation

Innovations in artificial intelligence, level design and gameplay meant that, by the late 1990s, a whole new style of first-person adventure was possible. Rather than having to blast their way through all opposition with brute force, players were – for the first time – given the option to avoid enemies altogether via stealth. Naturally, the first experience to have this treatment applied to it was the thrill of low-key British shoplifting, in Broken Harpsichord's *Petty Thief*. The game tells the tale of a nihilistic teenager called Gary, whose expertise in minor larceny sees him tasked with lifting a series of pathetic objects from a succession of increasingly well-guarded shops. The means by which he accomplishes his thieving – or as Gary calls it, "clever buying" – are as ingenious as they are varied. At times, it is as simple as stuffing burgers into the arm of a coat behind a fake hand, while later levels involve Gary releasing a dying fox into a shoe shop as a distraction, or impersonating a "government cigarette inspector" in a late night off-license. Perhaps the game's most challenging feature, however, is its deafening moral blankness. Way into the late-game, the player is strung along with the belief that Gary's pilfering is part of some grander plan; messages scrawled in graffiti suggest a greater power is watching him, and foreshadowing implies his plundering is part of a ritual to summon an ancient trickster god. But this is not the case. Gary just loves nicking things, and the game's final revelation is that the whole story is the fabrication of his defence lawyer, trying to get him acquitted on grounds of poor mental health. In this context, Gary's final mission – to steal the judge's wig before he's sentenced to a year in a Youth Offender's Institute – is bittersweet indeed.

VERDICT

Inventive, well-written and difficult without being maddening, *Petty Thief* showed what was possible when games sidestepped convention. It says a lot that in a year of big budget shooters, 1997's most exciting moment in videogaming would be snatching four cans of dog food from under the nose of a Tesco security guard.

"AT TIMES, IT IS AS SIMPLE AS STUFFING BURGERS INTO THE ARM OF A COAT BEHIND A FAKE HAND."

5 SNEAKY STEALTH CLASSICS

01 HOOT COLLECTOR // Unusual Pastimes, 2003

This web-based flash game, wildly popular among youths and fools, featured a goblin creeping through a twilit pastel realm, trying to get really really close to different kinds of owls in order to collect their hoots in a magical flask. At the end of the game, players could download an executable file which would irreversibly replace all windows system sounds with the hoots they had collected. As a result, the sound of the summer was relentless hooting, as parents desperately tried to clean the owl sounds out of their family PCs, only to be presented with endless, hoot-prompting error messages.

02 THE BLEND JUSTIFIES THE BEANS // Glass Sandwich Productions, 2013

One of the rare instances where the premise of a game lived up to the pun in its title, *Beans* featured notorious political theorist Nicollò Machiavelli, who, after making a terrible bargain with a mischievous imp, is trapped in the body of a Barista in a modern day Seattle coffee shop. He soon discovers that, in order to return to 1527, he must complete a ritual involving the fatal poisoning of one hundred customers. To achieve this feat without being caught, it's up to the founder of political science to use every trick he learned in the ruthless world of renaissance Italy, and come up with a few new ones besides.

03 DINNER GIT // Sorrowful Paul's House of Entertainment, 2017

While it was more a one-off art piece than a mass market hit, *Dinner Git* surely deserves a podium place in the history of stealth games. Played by one person at a time, this VR experience was set up in the kitchen of an upscale London restaurant, and linked users to a tiny drone equipped with a telescopic fork, hovering in the dining room next door. Players were tasked with sneaking around the dimly-lit room, plucking choice morsels from the plates of wealthy diners without being apprehended, then bringing them back to the control station to be sampled. Waiters were in on the ruse, and would frequently distract customers in order to facilitate the yoinking of oysters and caviar.

04 THE APE'S GRAPES // Electric Triumphs, 2008

Part of Electric Triumph's *Grapes of Wrath* series of games themed around fruit and anger, *The Ape's Grapes* gave players the role of a peckish zookeeper, hoping to pinch some lovely grapes from the corner of the chimps' den after hours. The chimps, which all begin the game asleep, were programmed with terrifyingly sophisticated AI – even the slightest rustle of footsteps on straw might cause one to stir in its slumber, or prompt the snapping open of a malevolent amber eye. And with only three tranquiliser darts to fire, there were only so many mistakes a player could make before being consigned to a horrific, screeching death beneath a dogpile of furious apes.

05 MORRIS ISLAND // Funworld, 2011

A private island in the Caribbean, a midsummer party thrown by a billionaire, and a crowd of Hollywood stars, rappers and supermodels protected by a private security force large enough to invade a country. What could possibly go wrong? Morris dancers: that's what. After some trust fund kid finds a haunted tambourine washed up on the beach and starts shaking it for a laugh, he is possessed by the Fool, a malevolent spirit of old England which had been imprisoned in the tambourine by warlocks three centuries previously. Blazing with the dark energy of Morris, the Fool capers about the island, turning everyone he dances with into Morris dancers, who then jig away and spread the infection themselves. Within hours the island is overrun by madness. Playing as the bodyguard of a rapper who falls victim to the plague, you must sneak through the chaos and escape by helicopter without being caught. Tense moments abound as you must blend into vast crowds of dancers, all the while moving as arrhythmically as possible so as to avoid getting Morrised.

36 BOYFIGHTS

HAND-HELD FIGHTER BUILT AROUND MANAGING LEVELS OF SHAME, FEAR AND PANIC IN ORDER TO OPTIMISE WILD FLAILING DURING PLAYGROUND SCRAPS.

YEAR
1997

GENRE
Adolescent Male Hierarchy /
Turn-Based Fighter

DEVELOPER
Fiasco Publishing

FORMAT
Game Boy Color

In the wake of landmark arcade release *Behind the Bins* (see p. 74), the fighting genre of the late 1990s was rife with games examining the concept of realism. From the no-frills, clinical battery of the *Microsoft Fight Simulator* series, to the PlayStation classic *Mokagi Masters*, in which characters' complete ignorance of martial arts led to fights full of clumsy headlocks and panic slapping, vérité was all the rage in simulated combat. Enter *Boyfights*, a release for the Game Boy Color which eschewed damage modelling and grappling physics altogether, in order to focus on the psychological elements of malcoordinated fighting. Set in a boundless, unsupervised playground, it put players in the shoes of a twelve-year-old boy, struggling to find his place in a world of nascent masculine aggression. The actual fighting in the game took place automatically: instead of selecting physical attacks, gameplay was about maintaining a mental state conducive to survival. For example, incoming insults could either be countered with lewd suggestions about an opponent's mother, or channelled straight into an inner rage pool, while the shock of being punched in the face could be directed straight back into the fists, or used to unlock a scream of fury to startle your foe and buy time. During the early game, *Boyfights* was mostly about enduring the predations of larger children, with choices of encounter limited by how much adrenaline you were willing to put into running away. As the player rose through the ranks of the tarmac battleground, however, play became less defensive, and more about picking fights that would secure your reputation as a pint-sized prizefighter. It could only end when everyone else in the playground was too scared to fight you, and your hatred turned against yourself.

VERDICT

Boyfights was as succinct a commentry on human power structures as it was as an enthralling turn-based fighter. The fluidity with which the game switched from being about survival to being about monstering weaker kids, without the core mechanics changing at all, was both deeply satisfying, and a sobering reflection on how bullies are created by bullying.

"PLAY BECAME LESS DEFENSIVE, AND MORE ABOUT PICKING FIGHTS THAT WOULD SECURE YOUR REPUTATION AS A PINT-SIZED PRIZEFIGHTER."

37

THEY CAN BREAK YOUR ARMS, YOU KNOW

SQUAD-BASED ACTION; LEAD A WADDLING GANG OF SWANS WITH BEEFY ARMS ON A QUEST TO SNAP EVERY HUMERUS IN TOWN.

YEAR
1998

GENRE
Waterfowl / Action-Adventure

DEVELOPER
Jungle Grandad Studios

FORMAT
PlayStation, PC Pentium MMX 120

We've all had the warning. Whether it came from a well-meaning grandmother, or that one friend who insists satsumas can cure blindness because they read it online, we know deep in our hearts that swans are imbued with the intrinsic power to break arms. It's a premise that spoils quickly when exposed to the light of reason, and yet it stays with us, evoking fear whenever we stray too near those grubby white devils of the lake. This game transports us to a world where this flimsy supposition is a fundament of reality; where we are the swans, and where the wet crack of human limbs is not just a possibility, but an imperative. Its hero is Cygnus Bonewreck, the subject of a hubristic attempt to create a war-ending bioweapon by sewing the arms of a bodybuilder onto the majestic body of a swan. Together with the rest of his experimental cohort – Savage Heinrich, Hassan the Breaker, and Tuulikki Joutsen, She Who Sends Men to Hospital – it's your mission to escape the military lab which created you, then break as many human arms as possible before you are recaptured. As the situation escalates, the humans send soldiers with increasingly well-protected arms, and you must make efficient use of your entire squad to unleash limb-busting combo attacks. Later, when you break into a hangar containing four gigantic prototype bird-mechs, the action moves to a whole new scale. After lashings of gruelling aerial combat, the action culminates in a duel with the Queen of England (traditionally the owner of all swans) piloting a twelve-armed combat exoskeleton. It's one of the most famous boss battles in gaming history, leading to perhaps the most daring ending ever – as Cygnus waddles over the flaming wreckage of the Queen's mech towards its prone pilot, flexing in anticipation of his final arm-snapping, the monarch stares straight at the camera and speaks. "None of this could actually happen," says the ruler of the UK, "because a swan is not capable of breaking a human arm." The credits roll in silence, and the player is left to contemplate the nature of received wisdom.

VERDICT

Blending several gameplay styles without any segment feeling like a weak link, *Arms* was a virtuoso debut for Jungle Grandad, and would set the studio on the road to its current position as a stalwart producer of triple-A game-changers. Swans still can't break your arms though.

"ESCAPE THE MILITARY LAB WHICH CREATED YOU, THEN BREAK AS MANY HUMAN ARMS AS POSSIBLE BEFORE YOU ARE RECAPTURED."

38 REGENCY OGRE DUELS

LUMBERING BRUTES IN POWDERED WIGS FACE OFF WITH FLINTLOCKS, WHILE BAFFLING FORMAL DANCE MINIGAMES ADD TO THE FUN.

YEAR
1998

GENRE
High Society / Ogres

DEVELOPER
Sausage Roll Games

FORMAT
PlayStation, PC Pentium II MMX 266

Usually when games are designed by committee, terrible things happen. But sometimes, just sometimes, you get *Regency Ogre Duels*. The game was the brainchild of Oliver Blood, who, after the *Moth Expert* fiasco in 1983 (see p. 20), had become something of an itinerant wunderkind in the business. Following the wild success of *Trollcopter* with Gigantic Developments, he was poached by Sausage Roll Games, where he proposed *Ogre Wars*, an action game about lumpen giants staggering around a blasted waste with crude firearms. Sausage Roll loved it, but were already dead set on putting out a game themed on romance and courtship in regency-era England. Blood balked at this, as the whole point of hiring him had been to replicate the 'burly monsters with guns' formula behind *Trollcopter*. Nevertheless, the board argued that after compromising genres on *Moth Expert*, he'd be able to do so again. Even though *Moth Expert* had sunk his company, Blood couldn't resist a challenge, and got to work. The result was a spellbinding nightmare where grimacing titans stalked each other through a crowded ballroom, trying to line up shots without being drawn into discussions on wig fashion. The atmosphere was unearthly: it was as if the game's human characters were incapable of perceiving the ogres in their midst, while the ogres, towering above them, kept their blazing eyes fixed only on each other. Finally, after years of producing violent schlock, Oliver Blood had created *art*.

Characters in *Regency Ogre Duels*:

Mr Grodnar, the Vicar: A beloved local figure despite his habit of eating nine children each midwinter.

Jane the Smasher: This season's most savage debutante, Jane stands twelve feet high and wields an iron-shod mammoth spine as a club.

Mr Fitzwilliam Zugdakk: A brooding bachelor who refuses to dance, preferring to eat offal from a wheelbarrow.

Lady Gristleblodd the Vast: Corsetted with the ribs of her enemies, Lady Gristleblodd is the central node of all the town's gossip.

Colonel Blugnak of the Blacktusk Legion: After coming home from the War, the once-kindly Colonel is beset by nightly visions of dragonfire.

VERDICT

If anything, the glaring discrepancy between the two social worlds in *ROD* added to the excitement – to be saved by the commencement of a formal dance right as an opponent levelled their blunderbuss at the back of your neck was a fist-pumping thrill every time.

Lord Burplap

Player 1

Lord Treup

oo
Fire!

"GRIMACING TITANS STALKED EACH
OTHER THROUGH A CROWDED BALLROOM,
TRYING TO LINE UP SHOTS."

39 LAW OF THE JUNGLE 2: PRIDE & PREJUDICE

CARTOON ANIMAL LEGAL PROCEDURAL PITTING AN ELEPHANT ATTORNEY AGAINST A JURY OF UNPLEASANT, SMALL-MINDED LIONS.

YEAR
1999

GENRE
Visual Novel / Megafauna / Law

DEVELOPER
Lounge Wizards North

FORMAT
Bandai WonderSwan

Although the *Law of the Jungle* series of all-animal legal RPGs would later become famous for its run of titles on the Game Boy Advance and Nintendo DS, the first two games in the series have been largely – and sadly – forgotten, due to having been released on the Bandai WonderSwan. This is a shame, as many connoisseurs of the series consider *LotJ 2* to have been the most charming of them all. Following on from *LotJ: Bear Den of Proof*, it continued the story of elephant defence attorney Sally Longnose, and her quest to acquit various zoo animals accused of wrongdoing. As its name might suggest, *Pride & Prejudice* presented a brand new challenge for Sally, as she came up against a jury of incredibly bigoted lions. The lions were utter bastards, and instantly assumed guilt of any non-feline animal, meaning an uphill struggle for Sally's clientele of amphibians, birds and insects. To make matters worse, this game saw the introduction of Judge Stripey, a supercilious tiger who would later become a fixture in the series, and who constantly pandered to the jury's outrageous behaviour. In the game's first case, where Sally defends a salamander accused of arson, the jury begins literally roaring during the examination of the first witness, and Stripey just laughs, before frisbeeing a steak across the courtroom to encourage them. The trial collapses, and the client is hurled straight into a well, casting Sally into a deep sadness. But you know what they say about elephants: they never let lions take the piss in a court of law. As such, the rest of the game alternated between standard courtroom scenes and night-time investigations, in which Sally discovered more about the jury's members in order to play on their weaknesses during upcoming trials. When you finally unlocked the dialogue options capable of shutting the lions right up, the satisfaction was enough to make you trumpet like the protagonist herself.

> ♫ Woooooah-oh, you're an elephant. You're a legal elephant. You're an elephant in a cartoon animal legal procedural. ♫
>
> – Advertising jingle for *Law of the Jungle 2*, sung to the tune of "Englishman in New York," by Sting.

VERDICT

Pride & Prejudice deserves to be remembered as Sally Longnose's standout outing: it's fun, it's easy to follow, and while it teaches you even less about animals than it does about the law, it's deeply fulfilling to play through.

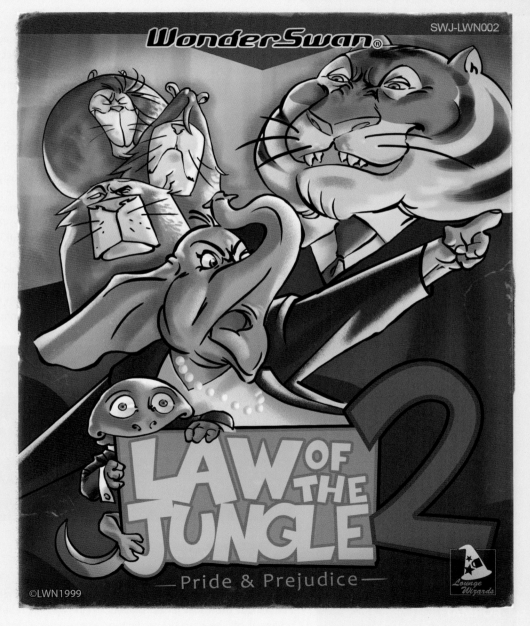

"THE LIONS WERE UTTER BASTARDS, AND INSTANTLY ASSUMED GUILT OF ANY NON-FELINE ANIMAL."

40 DEEP DISCOMFORT RACING

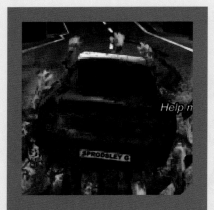

RACE THINGS THAT LOOK LIKE CARS, BUT WHICH GET REALLY UPSETTING IF YOU LOOK AT THEM TOO CLOSELY, IN THIS HIGH-OCTANE BODY HORROR DRIVING SIM.

YEAR
1999

GENRE
Body Horror / Racing

DEVELOPER
Jolly Bludgeon

FORMAT
PC Pentium III 450

"Help me… please." It's so quiet you think you've imagined it at first; just a whisper beneath the cheery butt-rock of the vehicle select screen. But then it comes again, and you can't ignore it. A desolate plea for help – muffled and metallic, but unmistakably human. You notice the bonnet of your chosen car flapping weakly, and mouse over it to investigate with a growing feeling of anxiety. Lifting the dented metal you reveal, in place of an engine, a dreadful mass of stretched skin and pulsing lumps. At its centre, a distorted face grimaces from behind wraparound shades. It strains for breath, oil leaking from withered lips, and wheezes the words "let's race." Welcome to *Deep Discomfort Racing*. This infamous title from Jolly Bludgeon, still banned in Germany, was simultaneously one of the best racers of its generation, and one of the most accomplished horror games ever made. It featured vehicles that performed like beautifully simulated sports cars, but which revealed vile biomechanical features upon closer inspection. Races, which took place in a deserted concrete hellscape, were incredibly tense affairs, with the dread of causing damage to your vehicle almost outpacing any desire to win. The game's answer to this was gorgeously sinister: on winning a race, vehicles would be dragged into a shed, from which a single gunshot would ring, putting them out of their misery and deleting them from the game's files. For players with even a shred of compassion, this made winning imperative, even if it eventually made the game unplayable.

Cars from *Deep Discomfort Racing:*

The Sprodsley 'Gorilla': Scampers on ungainly human arms, shrieking in confused terror.

Batford Motor Co. 'Tryhard': Grunts and pants in agony. Engine compartment nailed shut.

Binkler & Snipe Excelsior: Buzzes like a dying fly, drips viscous grey fluid from seams.

Munglesfield 'Witch Blood' Turbo: Tyres made of teeth. Engine bleeds. Mumbles apologies.

VERDICT

It says a lot about *DDR* that winning the game meant deleting it one piece at a time. For all but the most jaded players, there was no relief more profound than finally having it off the hard drive, despite what an excellent racing game it was.

"A DISTORTED FACE GRIMACES FROM BEHIND WRAPAROUND SHADES. IT STRAINS FOR BREATH, OIL LEAKING FROM WITHERED LIPS, AND WHEEZES THE WORDS 'LET'S RACE.'"

5 ODD RACING GAMES

While *Deep Discomfort Racing* was rare for being technically near-perfect at the same time as being profoundly weird, the last twenty years have seen plenty of racers that only managed the latter. Here are five of the more left-field entries into the usually straight-laced genre of people competing to make things go quickly:

01 AMBULANCE CHASERS // Computer Titans, 2002

In this bitter satire of the legal profession, players took on the role of personal injury lawyers, sprinting through the streets of a haggard commuter town in cheap suits. The goal was to chase down a jaunty cartoon ambulance, which spewed grubby coins from its rear doors as it sped merrily along. The more coins you collected, the more inhuman you became – as a race progressed, players would degenerate into hairless, clammy-skinned gollums, loping on all fours while hissing for money.

02 APE SUIT RACERS // Digital Jamboree, 2016

This lovable oddity was part racing game, part MMO, and part social experiment. Run from servers that were only online for an hour each week, it gathered thousands of players together at once, then set them loose in a simulated city wearing cheap gorilla costumes. A sort of anarchic marathon would ensue, as only one in every hundred players could see what direction the finish line lay in, and it was up to the rest to identify who knew what they were doing. The winner of each week's race would be sent four crates of bananas in real life, and everyone had a marvellous time.

03 CLOWN CARS // Large Yak Games, 2012

Merging the fun of cartoonish racing with the tactical depth of the squad-based strategy genre, *Clown Cars* saw players select a roster of clowns, before ramming them all into a comically small vehicle and heading online to race their friends. Different clowns offered different bonuses and special skills, from the ability to make cars jump, to weapons such as oil squirters and custard pie catapults. A surprisingly complex metagame evolved, as players discovered synergies the developers had never even imagined – just three months after release, someone managed to crash Large Yak's servers by selecting a clown team that allowed its car to break the sound barrier while exponentially increasing in mass.

04 SUPER NEW LABOUR KART // The UK Government, 1998

Perhaps the only example of a purely recreational game coming out of the public sector, this weirdly high-end production was a joy to play, despite raising some very serious questions indeed about why on earth it had received taxpayer funding. It featured the members of Tony Blair's inaugural 1997 cabinet, going hell for leather on go-karts through a colourful landscape themed on the decline of British socialism. Each had their own characteristics: John Prescott was slow to accelerate but delivered a brutal right hook, while Gordon Brown had superb top speed, but often spun off on corners.

05 WALRUS BIKES // Burlycom, 1994

Walrus Bikes was an absolute 16-bit shitshow. Playing as a human with a bucket of fish, it was your job to coax your trusty walrus friend up a mountain on its BMX, while tossing rotten fish to opposing walruses in order to discourage them. Gameplay wasn't bad, but good Lord was it slow – just getting to the start line could take fifteen minutes, and with no save capability, it was a rare race indeed that ever made it to the chequered flag.

2000 TO 2005

41 DANCE DANCE INDUSTRIAL REVOLUTION

MULTIPLE PLAYERS DANCE TO A POUNDING BEAT IN ORDER TO GENERATE THE RESOURCES NEEDED TO MECHANISE AGRARIAN SOCIETY.

YEAR
2000

GENRE
History / Rhythm

DEVELOPER
Tsunami

FORMAT
Arcade, PlayStation 2

Although it was never a widespread fixture in arcades due to its elaborate peripherals and extraordinary play length, *DDIR* has become renowned as both a mind-blowing multiplayer experience and a sobering history lesson. Featuring a room-sized, pressure sensitive dance mat printed with a map of the British Isles, the game invited groups of players to explore the industrialisation of early modern society through the medium of dance. Sticking to the rhythm would generate resources in the locations hit by players' feet, which in turn would build up cities onscreen, and gradually unlock more complex dance instructions. Play started slow, with simple rural prancing around a detachable maypole, and plastic turnips to brandish as tokens of agricultural output. After a series of intermediary coal-themed stages (and a woefully out of place mine cart level), players had a chance to change costumes and take a breather, before heading into the thundering drum 'n' bass lunacy of the industrial age. With each successive in-game decade taking more and more man-hours to get through, more and more players needed to be drafted in: while the early 1700s were easily achievable with two players, reaching the turn of the 19th century with any less than four was practically inviting exhaustion. Indeed, by the apex of the Victorian age, in a grim nod to social reality, the game required up to a dozen people to dance on the spot for hours on end, while the heaviest person at the party sat on London drinking wine. Completion often came unexpectedly, with the frantic beat of the music switching abruptly to the Last Post, and the screen fading to an image of a field of poppies. When the bugles stopped, players would be left with aching shins and drinks still in their hands, contemplating the dreadful cost of what they had achieved. It was pretty heavy stuff.

VERDICT

DDIR somehow managed to stretch the cheery play-style of a party game over the monolithic bones of history itself. With play times often exceeding 24 hours, it was certainly not to be undertaken lightly – as one reviewer famously commented, "*DDIR* is at once a marathon *and* a sprint." Nevertheless, as any veteran of its completion will tell you, it was a near life-changing experience to play, and remains a landmark fixture at history conventions and raves alike.

"EXPLORE THE INDUSTRIALISATION OF EARLY MODERN SOCIETY THROUGH THE MEDIUM OF DANCE."

42 LIZARD DESIGNER PRO: MILLENNIUM EDITION

RUSHED RELEASE WITH LIMITED FEATURES; YOU CAN'T EVEN GIVE THE LIZARDS TAILS, SO THEY'RE JUST THIN DRY FROGS REALLY.

YEAR
2000

GENRE
Herpetology / CAD

DEVELOPER
Scaly Software

FORMAT
PC Celeron II 766

As we look sheepishly back on the turn of the millennium, it's hard to remember why everyone got so excited about what was – let's face it – an arbitrary number with three zeroes in it. Nevertheless, the zeitgeist had it that the future was here, and every marketeer worth their salt dived at the opportunity like hounds to a trough of sausages. This resulted in some spectacularly empty releases in the world of software, of which *Lizard Designer PRO: ME* was perhaps the most emblematically shite. The thing was, the original *Lizard Designer* had only been released in 1999, and had conclusively met the needs of the herpetological planning community: it had a great interface, a superb library of reptile bits, and even a charming minigame based on leaping for flies. Even so, developers Scaly Software couldn't resist the chance to make a quick buck, and so rushed out this utter dog egg of an update in just eight months. Early hype promised a whole new rendering engine and rafts of new features including the 'lizard wizard' AI design assistant, and an online display realm called ReptileHaus. In very short order, however, Scaly realised just how much it had over-promised, and features began dropping like unpopular princes at a renaissance banquet. By June of 2000, with the project already three months overdue, the company realised the millennium hype was fading fast, and so decided to cut their losses and release. The game landed like a cow turd on a hot day, to instant rage from buyers. The new graphics made the game look as if it had been released five years before its predecessor, with textures that appeared to have been produced by pissed kids, and lizards that crawled lovelessly around in twitching circles. You couldn't load anything bigger than an iguana without bluescreening your PC, and the library of lizard bits was woeful, with only three kinds of tongues and no tails at all. A launch event at Stuttgart Zoo was cut short by protesters dressed as skinks, and Scaly folded less than a week later, as it emerged CEO Erhardt Schlanger had done a runner to Brazil with half the firm's cash.

VERDICT

LDP:ME lived on only as shovelware, bulking out CDs on the cover of subpar computing magazines. Nevertheless, thanks in part to a recent revival of sarcastic YouTube playthroughs, it has been remembered with a certain degree of nostalgia as an icon of millennial hubris.

"YOU COULDN'T LOAD ANYTHING BIGGER THAN AN IGUANA WITHOUT BLUESCREENING YOUR PC."

43 PUB FIGHT ARCHITECT

Somewhere at the end of the 1990s, developers realised that fans of simulation games didn't necessarily need any end condition to work towards – they were happy enough to muck around with the parameters of a pocket reality and see what mayhem they could cause. If said mayhem happened to cause needless distress to simulated human beings, then all the better. *Pub Fight Architect* began life as *Happy Hour*, a strategy game about running a successful bar. It soon dawned on the programmers, however, that the most fun to be had in the game was in stacking up tensions between patrons and then tipping them over the edge into fisticuffs. All constructive elements of the game were scrapped, in favour of giving players control over the psychological makeup of drinkers, the positioning of environmental elements, and the incursion of crisis events. For example, one could fill a city bar to bursting point with hedge fund managers, plant a kilo of cocaine in the centre of the room beneath a sleeping cage fighter, and then have fourteen glowering farmers march out of the toilets two minutes into the simulation, at the same moment as a fire breaks out behind the bar. The only limits were the player's imagination, and the number of flying pint glasses the game could render at once.

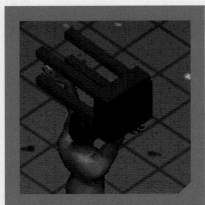

SANDBOX GAME WHERE YOU DESIGN A PUB AND PATRONS, THEN INJECT RANDOM EVENTS TO CAUSE A PERFECT STORM OF NEEDLESS RAGE.

YEAR
2000

GENRE
Disorder / Sandbox

DEVELOPER
No Solutions Entertainment

FORMAT
PC P4 1.4

Playable pubs:

The Broken Arms: Run-down cockney boozer, relocated inside a hospital out of a sense of ghastly inevitability.

The Shoe & Money: Haunt for shark-visaged city boys, with a balcony overlooking the grey Thames.

The Man's Blood: Eerie country pub complete with stuffed, snarling animals and paintings of sneering gentry.

The King's Fists: Flat-roofed, wipe-clean death pub with backroom dog arena.

The Slug & Email: Savage local reopened as a gastropub, but frequented by the same old peg-toothed gargoyles as before.

Ye Olde Dead Catte: Dingy, mahogany-clad failure saloon where the clientele of broken-lifed businessmen have faces meltier than the candles in the port bottles.

VERDICT

For a game so brutally themed, *PFA* was oddly relaxing – there was considerable catharsis in seeing a disagreement over a spilled pint escalate into a 40-man bloodbath, and it was arguably a more effective de-stressing tool than an actual pub.

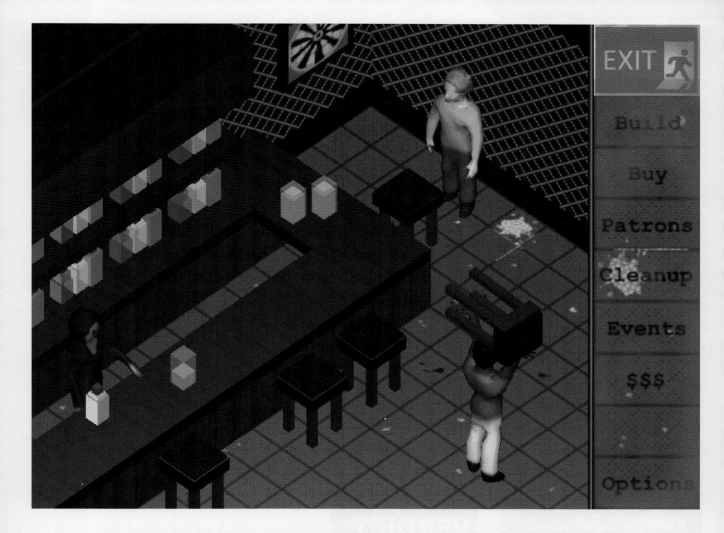

"THE MOST FUN TO BE HAD IN THE GAME WAS IN STACKING UP TENSIONS BETWEEN PATRONS AND THEN TIPPING THEM OVER THE EDGE INTO FISTICUFFS."

44

PISSED BUSHIDO

FPS ACTION: STRUGGLE TO PLAY AS A SAMURAI WHO IS UTTERLY, FALLING-DOWN, ENDGAME SHITFACED 24 HOURS A DAY.

YEAR
2001

GENRE
Trying To Stand Up / Martial Arts

DEVELOPER
Heavy Times

FORMAT
Xbox, PlayStation 2

Despite ostensibly sharing a theme of alcohol-fuelled violence with *Pub Fight Architect*, one could scarcely find a game with a more distinct heritage than *Pissed Bushido*. The game's genesis came when Japanese games artist Kaori Murayama read about Zui Quan, the 'drunken fist' school of Chinese martial arts, and set out to design a game exploring the concept through the lens of her own nation's Bushido culture. Working with martial artists and historians, she took Zui Quan's fluid movements – which simulated the appearance of drunkenness despite the crystal-sharp focus of the practising warrior – and applied them to the sword-based styles of the samurai, creating a whole new fictional fighting style in the process. When the game was taken on by US developer Heavy Times, however, a crude misunderstanding completely shat on this intriguing premise. "So basically," summarised Heavy Times CEO Jerry Boffer, after a detailed presentation by Murayama and a swordmaster, "it's about a samurai who's completely blotto all the time. Perfect. Let's get it done by Christmas." And so, to Murayama's dismay, that's what they did. The work that emerged wasn't bad by any means – it was easily one of the top commercial releases of 2001. It was just... such a waste of potential. Featuring Sakai Takatora, a samurai warrior who spends his life thoroughly busted on rice wine, the game was a messy series of duels with pretty much everything that came within swinging distance. The controls were deliberately wankered, so it was hard enough just keeping Takatora upright, let alone fending off the swarm of samurai, demons and blurry visions that were possibly attacking him. All too often, players would suffer self-inflicted deaths, impaled while trying to deal with pieces of furniture that had given them a nasty look, while combos would often be broken by unskippable bouts of dry heaving. For all its fundamental problems, nobody could say *Pissed Bushido* wasn't challenging.

VERDICT

Despite the utter bungling of its original premise by clueless US execs, *Pissed Bushido* evolved into something beautiful in its own right. It wasn't an easy game, either to play or to comprehend, but in terms of a game to play after coming back from the pub after a proper ale ruining, nothing has since come close.

"A SAMURAI WARRIOR WHO SPENDS HIS LIFE THOROUGHLY BUSTED ON RICE WINE."

45 NIGHTS IN ARMOUR

GUIDE SIR TRANCEALOT, THE RAVE KNIGHT, THROUGH AN ELECTRO ODYSSEY IN THIS RHYTHM- AND MELODY-DRIVEN PLATFORM BELTER.

YEAR
2001

GENRE
Massive Beats / Platform RPG

DEVELOPER
Sophie Leung / Bin Planet

FORMAT
Nintendo 64

Like many stories from the chivalric tradition it riffed on, *Nights in Armour* began with a warrior inspired to a quest by a holy vision. The warrior was IT technician Sophie Leung, and the holy vision was a DJ in a cheap plastic knight's helmet, manning the decks at a warehouse rave on the outskirts of Cardiff. Leung was just coming up on a soldier dose of MDMA, when this figure from yore dropped the harpsichord segment from an Orbital record, slammed on the strobes, and raised his foam sword into the air. Leung sank to her knees at the grandeur of the moment, and fell into a deep, rapturous appraisal of the entire Arthurian tradition as the beats thundered on. The next day she quit her job, spent all her savings on electronic equipment, and vowed not to rest until she had recreated the moment in art. Four years of work later, Leung sent a demo of *Nights in Armour* to publisher Bin Planet, who proceeded to fish out the biggest cheque they could find in order to snap it up. Quite simply, she had smashed it – she had fused the concepts of knights and dance music, via the medium of a retro RPG/platformer, and done the concept more justice than Batman could fit into the world's biggest courtroom. The game featured Sir Trancealot, a paladin ablaze with glowsticks, who battled through a twilight realm in constant pursuit of gigantic tunes. It was slickly animated despite its retro aesthetic, and mixed traditional trudge & slash segments with interludes of avant-garde brilliance: in one level, Trancealot becomes an actual castle, and must endure 1,000 years of sped-up weather and sieges before he can return to his human form. And the soundtrack – every note composed by Leung herself – was mind-shattering. Every step the Rave Knight took in time with the music increased his power, while successful sword strokes would add euphoric synth riffs to the soundscape. Words can't do justice to the magic that was skewering a trainful of goblins on the Breakbeat Express level. And the final boss battle – a first person DJ duel with the undead King of Disco, was exactly as fun as it sounds.

VERDICT

From the synthesised voice bellowing "TUNE!" over its title screen to the goblins with whistles and jester's hats in the credits, *Nights in Armour* was a masterpiece.

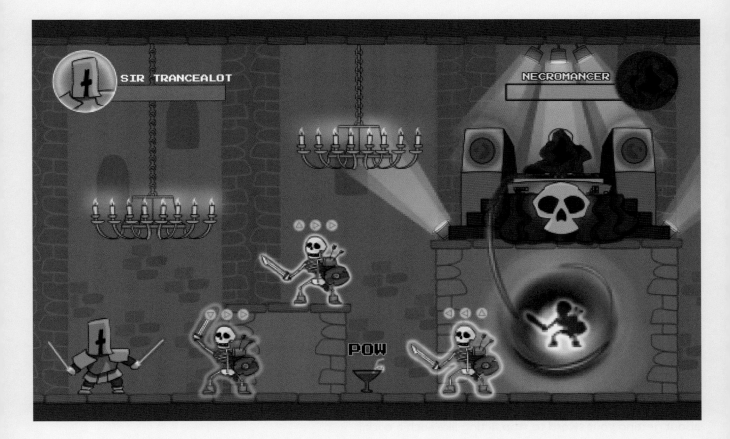

"A PALADIN ABLAZE WITH GLOWSTICKS, WHO BATTLED THROUGH A TWILIGHT REALM IN CONSTANT PURSUIT OF GIGANTIC TUNES."

TEN NEARLY FORGOTTEN RPGs

The 2000s saw an explosion in RPGs of many kinds, as branching narrative, deep dialogue and character customisation became *de rigueur* across the genres. While some are famous enough to be featured elsewhere in this collection, here are ten largely hidden gems, and one stinker, from the storied history of RPG gaming:

01 HORSEPLAY // Arcadian Distractions, 2005

In this profoundly frustrating RPG, you play as a frustrated Broadway director who must direct a series of famous plays using all-horse casts. Looking after the physical and emotional wellbeing of the horses is hard enough, while the acting segments are nearly impossible until you get the hang of what to whisper in the ears of your long-faced actors.

02 LOCAL COUNCIL LAUGHS // Empires of Amazement, 1999

In this game, featuring an ornery bastard with a job for life in a run-down London council tax office, it's your job to make life as inconvenient and miserable as possible for your colleagues using only a rotary dial phone and a limited set of stationery. While it's never been proved, aficionados suspect developers Empires of Amazement were the same mysterious figures who produced 1985's similarly themed *Work Kitchen Anecdote Bastard* (p. 32).

03 WORLD OF PIGS // Digital Garys, 2008

Garbage MMO. Play as a pig. Eat some parsnips. Fail to interact with other pigs. Cancel your subscription. Rubbish.

04 BASTARD SWORD // Hammerthumbs Entertainment, 2013

A young woman sets out on a quest for revenge in the ruins of a post-apocalyptic world – but there's a problem. Her sword is a complete and utter *arsehole*. It never shuts up. It's constantly naysaying everything you do, and there's nothing you can do to get rid of it. In time, the game becomes less about a quest for revenge, and more about getting your sword to stop acting like such a cock.

05 RUFF JUSTICE // Alleyway Badboys, 2010

Set in a gorgeously vibrant recreation of Elizabethan London, this open world adventure starred playwrights-turned-cops Bill Shakespeare and Ben Jonson, roaring around the theatres, taverns and bearpits of their day in a wooden muscle car. Voice acting and dialogue was top-notch, with the hustle of 1980s Brooklyn translated perfectly into the early modern vernacular, while the plot – which involved Shakespeare writing *Hamlet* in order to expose a drug dealer at its opening night – was inspired. Should have been a bigger hit.

06 A GRAHAM OF PHONES // Turbosoft Developments, 2015

This quick-fire RPG sets you off on a straightforward footing – you are a man called Graham, working in a Scottish call centre for an energy company. You take calls, choose dialogue options, and chat with your colleagues. But when Graham begins taking calls from a dying king in a fantasy realm, he must first question the integrity of his mind, and then the boundaries of his reality.

07 MY LIFE AS A BOOZER // Sprodsley Creations, 2001

Telling the tale of Sid, a man who becomes a pub as a result of a tragic accident, this combined RPG/management sim features a side-on view of the possessed facility, in which Sid can nudge the staff of the pub to carry out his bidding in the physical world. Sparking romances and good times within him will strengthen Sid, giving him new powers, while fights and arrests will damage his mind to the point where he eventually loses his sentience altogether, ending the game.

08 IGNORANCE KNIGHT // Code Blop, 2017

Code Blop presented players with a unique dilemma in this hugely underrated open world masterpiece. While the setting was incredibly detailed, containing more lore and dialogue text than the entire *Lord of the Rings* series, immersing yourself in it came at a terrible price. Sir Ignacio, the hero of the piece, begins as an unstoppable warrior, but grows weaker with every moment in which the game detects you reading or listening to background information. Even by skipping through dialogue and ignoring all books, it's hard to reach the final boss – a librarian – with the ability to even raise a sword.

09 DESERT GIT // Perry Gurnard, 1986

While not many old school text adventures can hold up against the triple-A titans of recent years, this single-developer classic from 1986 is among them. Playing a capering fool with nothing better to do, your only goal is to travel across a sprawling desert, causing slight inconvenience to wildlife and fellow travellers. Admittedly, there's not much there in the way of win conditions, but play itself is weirdly liberating.

10 REVERSE BEASTMASTER 2 // Rancid Principle Software, 2012

In this expansive fantasy RPG, you play a powerful barbarian who must constantly acquiesce to the whims of animals. Trying to find a queen's lost sceptre in a distant dungeon? Tough, fucko; a snail just told you to go fetch a lettuce, so now you're doing that instead. Maddening.

46 GORILLA SKY JUSTICE

LAND A CHINOOK FULL OF ENRAGED SILVERBACKS AT A SERIES OF PLACES WHERE BAD THINGS HAPPEN, AND REVEL IN THE CONSEQUENCES.

YEAR
2001

GENRE
Primal Rage / Strategy

DEVELOPER
BeastMode Entertainment

FORMAT
PC P4 1.3, Xbox,
PlayStation 2

Have you ever looked at the state of the world and, for a single dark moment, wondered how many problems you could solve if you only had access to a transport helicopter packed with furious gorillas? If so, you have probably played *Gorilla Sky Justice*. This wasn't a complicated game – but then, it never needed to be. The strategic portion saw you running a secret mountaintop gorilla breeding facility, and was all about expanding your ape stables and upgrading your choppers. Then, when alerted to grim goings on – an arms fair, for example, or the dumping of nuclear waste in a lake – it was time to scramble. You'd choose a vehicle, load up your gorillas, and head to the scene. This was where the game really came into its own – missions occurred in slow motion, with one to three apes (depending on upgrades) emerging from the transport craft every five seconds. You could point them in the right direction on their way out, and issue basic commands, but largely it was a case of sitting back and watching the mayhem unfold. The more justice you delivered (moves such as throwing villains through plate glass windows scored combo bonuses), the more points you scored, and the more you could upgrade your base. There was a twist, however – beyond a certain point, governments and underground groups would begin offering huge sums of cash to deploy gorillas on their behalf, all in the name of 'solving problems.' When you eventually caved, and found yourself dumping thirty silverbacks in a monastery to silence a political dissident for money, you realised that *you had become the problem*.

While *GSJ*'s initial locations were great, a huge modding community built up around the game, creating custom scenarios of their own. Fan-made arenas for the game include:

Tory Party Conference: Heseltine's up to speak, but is drowned out by the thudding of rotors...

Waterloo Station: Impatient rush hour businessmen learn a deadly lesson about pushing and shoving...

Cambridge May Ball: An opulent toast to another year of success. But what's that in the sky...?

VERDICT

While *GSJ*'s endgame proved that gorillas aren't the solution to everything, its sobering message on the nature of power was undermined by the sheer glee of thrashing things with apes. In a world where many feel so powerless, who can resist the cathartic thrill of *Gorilla Sky Justice*?

"LARGELY IT WAS A CASE OF SITTING BACK AND WATCHING THE MAYHEM UNFOLD."

47 NIGHT BUS ADVENTURES

A LONE WANDERER ATTEMPTS TO CROSS LONDON AT MIDNIGHT, USING EVERY TRICK IN THE BOOK TO WARD OFF PERIL ON THE LAWLESS DECKS OF THE NIGHT BUSES.

YEAR
2002

GENRE
Public Transport / Tactical RPG

DEVELOPER
Game Kings

FORMAT
PC P4 1.8

It's 3am on the N9, and things are about to kick off. Four teenagers in the depths of an acid trip have made their way to the top deck, adding to an already tense standoff between two groups of football fans, and a gentleman of the street has begun to roar downstairs. Your supplies are limited – all that's left in your pack is three cans of warm lager and a bag of hot wings – but somehow you must broker a truce. This is *Night Bus Adventures*, and you are the Roadman, a mysterious ranger figure, tasked with roaming the city's nocturnal routes and maintaining a semblance of order. The game begins at the stroke of midnight and ends at 6am – in that time, you must make your way from West Ruislip all the way across the sprawl of the capital to Orpington, in the far Southeast. The journey can involve up to nine bus journeys, depending on how wisely you choose your routes, with each bringing its own share of randomly generated NPCs, crisis events and gameplay modifiers. Play revolves around using items and skills to placate, subdue or trick opponents before they can flip out: since each incident of violence can add an hour to the Roadman's journey and damage him for the rest of the game, physical solutions are almost always a last resort. While changing buses, you have a limited window of time to scavenge 24 hour off-licences and petrol stations for new items, but pickings become slimmer and slimmer as the game goes on. Sometimes it's worth the risk of taking on friendly NPCs as followers – they may have rare inventory items or vital pay-as-you-go phone credit – but it's not worth getting attached to them. Put too much hope in the old man who joins the bus at Acton Town Hall, and you'll be devastated when he disappears forever in search of a kebab, just an hour later. Misfortune abounds in *Night Bus Adventures*, and defeat is often inevitable from the start – but that makes victory all the sweeter when you finally manage a successful transit.

VERDICT

With brutally realistic dialogue and a diamond-hard resource conservation metagame, *NBA* was incredibly unforgiving of mistakes. Yet with random elements making every playthrough unique, it was a challenge you would find yourself tackling again and again – while as few as one in ten playthroughs ended with seeing dawn in Kent, it was worth it every time.

"MISFORTUNE ABOUNDS IN *NIGHT BUS ADVENTURES*, AND DEFEAT IS OFTEN INEVITABLE FROM THE START."

48 MONOPOLY: AFTERMATH

EPIC FPS SET IN THE FRAGILE HOPE OF A POST-CAPITALIST WORLD, WHERE THE TOP HAT, IRON, RACECAR AND TERRIER MUST FIND NEW PURPOSE.

YEAR
2002

GENRE
Post-Capitalist / FPS

DEVELOPER
Champions of Winning

FORMAT
Xbox

"It's all fun and games until the money runs out." So begins the weary narration of the Top Hat, as *Monopoly: Aftermath*'s opening cinematic begins to roll. As the voiceover continues, we are introduced to a world ruined by the consequences of the Monopoly rule-set: monolithic hotels occupy every inch of land, while jails creak with the bones of debtors. Mouldering stacks of money line the streets, made useless by hyperinflation to the point where it was only fit for building barricades. It's been years since anyone collected money for passing Go, and yet the warlords who rule the citadel of Community Chest still hold daily beauty contests for its desperate citizens. It is a broken world, into which you venture as the Pieces: a band of pewter golems, originally built to maintain order, but now freed from their programming and determined to raise a better world from the ashes. The Top Hat, voiced by Sigourney Weaver, is wracked with guilt over its former role, while the Terrier (Jack Black) is loyal yet profoundly sad. Ving Rhames' Iron smoulders with frustration at the injustices of the world around it, while the Racecar (Donald Sutherland) displays a disturbing wistfulness for the excesses of the old regime. Nevertheless, despite their differences, the Pieces come to realise that their only hope of creating a better society is to band together and use their powers as a team. As such, the player can switch between the Pieces for different types of missions – while the Terrier excels at stealth, for example, the Racecar is peerless for traversing the stretches of wasteland in between the colour-coded districts of the Board. It's just as well, because when it comes to taking down Rich Uncle Pennybags, the moustachioed overlord of the wastes, you'll need to have mastered all of their playstyles.

Besides the four main Pieces, a range of other monopoly tokens make cameo appearances in the game:

The Wheelbarrow (Whoopi Goldberg): A veteran who conceals their pain by making others laugh.

The Boot (Mark Hamill): Despite seeming bitter and resentful, it can't bear to see innocents suffer.

The Cannon (Ellen DeGeneres): A condemned war machine with a ruined mind, but a kind heart.

VERDICT

Thanks to its cinematic stylings, A-list voice cast and poignant writing, *Monopoly: Aftermath* is a game that will stay with you long after the final roll of the dice.

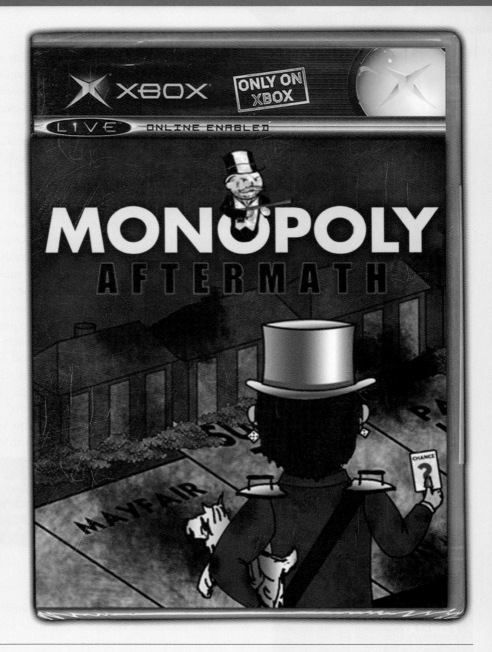

"IT'S ALL FUN
AND GAMES
UNTIL THE
MONEY RUNS
OUT."

49 A NORMAL LIFE

TENSE ACTION: MANAGE THE DEMANDS OF FAMILY LIFE WHILE SECRETLY KEEPING NINE RAGING BOXERS IMPRISONED IN YOUR SHED.

YEAR
2002

GENRE
False Imprisonment / Strategy

DEVELOPER
Hard Times Productions

FORMAT
PC P4 2.4, PlayStation 2

Meet Kevin Bread, a father of three with a job in IT, a decent golf handicap, and a shed full of very angry men. Kevin's story begins on a Friday, when a dawn phone call explains that several professional boxers have been locked in his garden shed by the mafia. If Kevin can maintain the situation until Sunday night, the caller says, the boxers will be removed and drowned, and Kevin will earn one million dollars. A deal is struck, and your weekend as a reluctant jailer proceeds as a tutorial introducing the basic mechanics of the game. Each day, Kevin is given a certain number of actions, which can be used to feed and water the boxers, reinforce the shed, and maintain the illusion of normalcy to your family. At first, things seem surprisingly achievable. Things take a turn, however, when Sunday night comes and goes without any sign of the mafia. Kevin is faced with a dilemma – does he let the boxers free and risk their wrath, or does he wait in the hope that the mysterious caller will get back in touch? With each day that passes, it gets harder to balance the maintenance of the boxers with the needs of Kevin's family, and the sportsmen become more infuriated. Some plead and some attempt to bargain, while others just go mad, smashing the walls and roaring. In time, the boxers turn on each other, bringing a grim new set of consequences to deal with. By the end of the first week, things get *dark*. The game has many different endings, but very few of them are happy – the longer things go on, the more you resent Kevin's initial decision, and the more you welcome his eventual fate. By the denouement of *A Normal Life*, gameplay is less about working towards Kevin's profit, and more about safeguarding his family against his terrible mistake.

"When are we getting out?" states a hard voice as you mash burgers with a fork to prepare the day's feed. "You know we'll kill you when we do," adds another, with cold sincerity. Your hands, like the walls of the shed, begin to shake.

– Dialogue from Day Four, *A Normal Life*

VERDICT

Masterfully balanced and powerfully written, *A Normal Life* is a game that will make you think twice before ever imprisoning a gang of professional fighters in your garden shed.

"WITH EACH DAY THAT PASSES, IT GETS HARDER TO BALANCE THE MAINTENANCE OF THE BOXERS WITH THE NEEDS OF KEVIN'S FAMILY."

50 MOULIN LUGE

RACY WINTER SPORTS SIM; AFTER THEIR CLUB SHUTS DOWN, A GANG OF CORSETED ENTERTAINERS SETS OUT FOR THE WINTER OLYMPICS.

YEAR
2003

GENRE
Cabaret / Winter Sports

DEVELOPER
Electroguff

FORMAT
Xbox, PlayStation 2

Once you got past the fact that it was essentially the 1993 film *Cool Runnings*, but with more garters and sequins, *Moulin Luge* was a real gem of a sports game. It told the story of a troupe of Parisian cabaret performers, who fall on hard times after their venue is arsonised by a bastard duke. Running out of cash, and wilting without their nightly variety shows, they are suffering an existential crisis until ageing courtesan Delphine sees a vision of a toboggan at the bottom of an absinthe bottle. Realising they have one *hell* of a pun on their hands, the ragtag ensemble vow there and then to master a range of sled-based sports and win gold for France at the 2002 Winter Olympics. The early game is mightily entertaining, and features the troupe's madcap training exercises on the steep streets of the Montmartre district. It is here they learn that frilly skirts and feather boas are a terrible, terrible idea for wear during high speed tobogganing, prompting a superb minigame about designing a more practical, yet still highly slinky, uniform for the team. Once they are kitted up and versed in the basics, their practice runs begin taking on more and more aspects of cabaret dancing, including horizontal interpretations of the can-can, and bobsleigh extravaganzas set to sexy French music. But the fun can't last forever – soon enough, the action moves to Salt Lake City, where the real competition begins. Unusually for a sports game, however, it's not all no-frills simulation – in between the daytime races, players guide the various performers through night-time RPG sequences, where they drink, cavort, and find mischief and romance in the Olympic Village. Whether they can eventually outcompete the steely-necked Alpine elite is a matter of player skill, and it's a damned good attempt at the game that manages even a single bronze medal. Nevertheless, winning the hearts of the world with the troupe's saucy antics on the ice is another matter, and makes for a much more rewarding play experience.

VERDICT

At once a rip-roaring winter sports sim and a heartwarming fish-out-of-water comedy, *Moulin Luge* managed to plant one exquisitely-heeled foot on each genre and throw glitter in the eyes of the gaming world. A beloved title.

"IT IS HERE THEY LEARN THAT FRILLY SKIRTS AND FEATHER BOAS ARE A TERRIBLE, TERRIBLE IDEA FOR WEAR DURING HIGH SPEED TOBOGGANING."

15 BALL-BUSTING SPORTS GAMES

From 1972's *Paddly Lads*, widely regarded as the first video game, right through to modern releases like *Mickey Heartscream's Infinite Baseball*, sport has been one of the core genres in gaming. Providing an instant arena for friendly competition without any need for setup, equipment or actual exercise, sports games are a perennial treat for people who care really hard about balls. Here are fifteen classics:

01 JOHN MADDEN'S FOOTBALL SERIES // Computery Arts, 1988-present

A whimsical tale about a man's beloved football, told over three decades. With each year the ball becomes more careworn and fragile; players cradle it like a precious, leathery egg.

02 QUANTUM PHYSICS ACID TRIP CRICKET 5 // The Reality Mill, 2016

Sense-of-self-melting cricket simulation set in the same moment as all previous entries in the series. Difficult, especially when Geoffrey Boycott begins whispering aphorisms about mortality.

03 INCREDIBLE HULK GOLF // Sleepy Geoffrey's Game Company, 2007

Maddening golf sim for the Nintendo Wii where anything but the lightest swing results in a crater and a ball hurtling towards the stars at an appreciable fraction of the speed of light.

04 IT MIGHT BE RUGBY // Code Fools, 2010

Rugby game designed according to instructions from 100 people who've never seen a game of rugby, given a pint of vodka each and asked to share a single microphone. There is a ball, at least.

05 BULLSEYE: OLYMPUS // Lagerboy Home Entertainment, 1995

Epic tribute to the classic UK darts show; mightily-girthed Midlanders take on the stature of Greek gods and hurl skyscraper-sized darts at human cities, using orbital mechanics for trick shots.

06 ANTICLIMACTIC BASKETBALL // Sorrowsports, 2004

Full of flashing lights, pumped-up music and razzle-dazzle – but dunks are accompanied by a dismal fanfare, a slow fade to grey, and the obliteration of all game data.

07 MECHANOID BATTLE CRICKET // Digital Chalice, 2014

A fledgling human empire meets a race of feral self-replicating machines around the ruins of a distant solar system, and challenges them to a test cricket match for control of mining rights.

08 MOON OLYMPICS // The Balti Brothers, 1999

Impossibly frustrating sports anthology where gravity is a fucking joke, javelins whistle off hopelessly into infinity, and the long jump takes ages. The weightlifting bits are cool, though.

09 FLICKERLAMP GHASTBALL // Dracula's Picnic Games, 2002

Sports horror game; you operate the sole functioning spotlight in a stadium where football teams insist on repeatedly playing fixtures at night despite an infestation of carnivorous ghouls. Working by sound cues, try to drive waves of monsters from the pitch with your sputtering beam before they can devour all the sportsmen.

10 THE MOLLUSC CHALLENGE // Eggvision Interactive, 1996

Very silly compilation of minigames from the makers of *Earthworm Gym* (p. 76); compete in the Snail Sprint, the Bivalve High Jump, Octopus Judo and more. Charming, invertebrate-based family fun.

11 ALL OR NOTHING BASKETBALL // Blasted Sergeant, 1997

Horrific arcade game where, after the match has passed an arbitrary time limit, players tear off their own heads to dunk instead of the balls provided. Gets very tense.

12 PETE SAMPRAS' TENNIS GAME // Pete Sampras, 1994

A tennis game entirely designed, programmed and voiced by tennis legend Pete Sampras. It's really not very good, but it was a spirited effort given the man's existing tennis commitments.

13 GIGAMECH FOOTBALL // Godbreaker Entertainment, 2017

A surprisingly accurate American football game where the pitch is a war-torn future city, the ball is a hydrogen bomb, and the players are 200ft tall diesel-powered war machines.

14 MILLENNIAL OLYMPICS // Old Rich White Man Games, 2016

Bitter sports collection coded by self-regarding, tabloid-reading bastards. Players get medals for losing, and the game begins sneering at you for not keeping the economy going if you refuse to bankrupt yourself with microtransactions.

15 BIKE POPE // Divine Interventions, 2001

Guide the pontiff through a 10,000 mile global odyssey, performing sick BMX trips while busting out benedictions on paupers. Combo tricks allow you to enshrine new dogma in church doctrine.

51 RECRUITMENT BARN 2051

TOP-DOWN MANAGEMENT SIM ABOUT FARMING SALESPEOPLE IN A WORLD WHERE HUMANITY HAS DESCENDED INTO A NIGHTMARE OF CHICKEN AND BANTER.

YEAR
2003

GENRE
Post-Apocalyptic Sales /
4X Strategy

DEVELOPER
Pixelgits

FORMAT
PC Athlon 2600+

In the grim darkness of the near future, there is only telesales. *Recruitment Barn 2051*, based on the novel of the same name, tasks players with building a battery farm for recruitment consultants, in a world reduced to the demented worship of modern business culture. At its heart are 'the lads,' the genderless, feral humans that staff your sales operation. You begin with four of them in a concrete cell, along with a single telephone and a hatchery for breeding the limbless, bird-derived food organisms called 'nandoes.' The more 'calls' the lads make (the telephone is made of solid plastic, and connects to nothing), the more commission you receive from the mysterious Shareholders, and the more you can expand. Gyms and sales training rooms come first, followed by operating theatres for creating the cyborg horrors known as Line Managers. Morale must be considered too – chemical plants can be built to refine Lynx Africa for the lads' hygiene, as well as crude hydroponic gardens for growing Bensons and Spliffs. As the lads grow rowdier you must build them an external Banter Yard, and in time a commissary known as a Spoons, where you feed them the crude intoxicant known as Jäger. Each lad has many stats – those which underperform can be pulped and mixed in with the nandoes, while the most successful can be promoted to the rank of Legend and used to browbeat their fellows into hitting the phones harder. Numbers can be swelled by transferring the DNA of your best lads into vast eggs, which can force-grow a six foot adult in less than a week. Every so often, a Shareholder will descend in a black hovercraft to check on your KPIs, and may grant sanctions or boons to your firm as a result. Eventually, with a large enough sales force, you can embark on a Night Out – a cross between a teambuilding activity and a crusade, where you raid other firms for resources and fresh genetic material. Conduct enough successful Nights Out and you will eventually be made a Shareholder yourself, unlocking *Recruitment Barn 2051*'s chilling endgame content.

VERDICT

RB2051's mix of resource management and base-building is so compelling that it's easy to forget the utter horror of its premise, and the suffering inflicted on the lads as the player grows in power. There's probably a message in there, but who cares – there's phones to be hit.

"A BATTERY FARM FOR RECRUITMENT CONSULTANTS, IN A WORLD REDUCED TO THE DEMENTED WORSHIP OF MODERN BUSINESS CULTURE."

52 GORILLIONAIRE!

OPEN WORLD CITY ADVENTURE, FEATURING A BANKRUPT WOMAN WHO TRANSFORMS INTO A MIGHTY, MONEY-WASTING GORILLA EVERY TIME SHE CLIMBS OUT OF DEBT.

YEAR
2003

GENRE
Problem Debt / Apes

DEVELOPER
BeastMode Entertainment

FORMAT
Nintendo Gamecube

Jane Silverback, the protagonist of *Gorillionaire!*, was easily one of the most memorable characters to emerge from the 2000s in video gaming. Despite being a prudent woman who will do anything to give her daughter a good life, she is perpetually broke. That's because ever since she was given a haunted coin by a zoo gorilla, Jane has been the victim of a dreadful curse – if she is ever out of debt, she transforms into GORILLIONAIRE, a gigantic ape with a pinstripe suit, a lust for life, and a profound lack of fiscal reckoning. Jane can only regain her human form once Gorillionaire's purchases – or the cost of the damage caused on his destructive commercial adventures – sink her deep back into debt. This Sisyphean existence is a constant struggle for Jane, as she constantly balances her duty to provide for Hannah with a burning desire *not to transform into a spendthrift gorilla*. The game follows Jane on her quest to understand, manage, and eventually lift her curse, while putting food on the table and dealing with the consequences of her simian rampages. Along the way, she faces several crises that threaten to drop her into enormous wealth, which provide huge dilemmas for the player. After all, while it's hard not to be compelled by Jane's predicament, it's also near-impossible to resist transforming into Gorillionaire, since the game's rampage gameplay is so utterly rhapsodic. Over time, the player must answer the gorillion dollar question: do they sacrifice consequence-free mayhem for the sake of resolving Jane's narrative, or embrace it and leave her in a perpetual state of uncertainty and exhaustion?

Some missions from *Gorillionaire!*

• Jane's friends take her to a casino, and she must cheat the house to make sure she loses.

• Jane is given 100 lottery tickets, and must get rid of them all before the draw is made.

• Gorillionaire gains a sponsorship deal, meaning his rampages actually earn him money.

• The death of an estranged grandfather leaves Jane in possession of a wildly profitable banana import company.

VERDICT

Not many games have managed to deliver madcap, car-throwing action alongside a sobering message about spending addiction, but *Gorillionaire!* did so by the shovelful. Possibly the most exuberantly bleak game ever made.

"A GIGANTIC APE WITH A PINSTRIPE SUIT, A LUST FOR LIFE, AND A PROFOUND LACK OF FISCAL RECKONING."

53 EVERY LITTLE HELPS

RTS/RPG HYBRID FEATURING THE STAFF OF A 24HR TESCO WHO ARE CONSCRIPTED TO CREW A COLOSSAL WAR MACHINE AT THE END OF TIME.

YEAR
2004

GENRE
Supermarket Management /
Real Time Strategy

DEVELOPER
Spiffing Games

FORMAT
PC P4 3.4

Following proudly in the footsteps of *Red Dwarf* and *Hitchhiker's Guide*, this game painted a story of profoundly British mundanity onto the sprawling canvas of time and space. It all starts reasonably enough: *ELH*'s tutorial introduces Tess Challenge, the manager of a massive Tesco, as she works to get it shut down for midnight on Christmas Eve. The game's people management mechanics are introduced gently, and all goes well despite Tess' demob-happy staff. Everything changes at 11.59pm, however, when a race of unknowable beings called the Krax contact Tess via a searing hole in reality. The Krax are rebels in a galaxy-spanning religious conflict billions of years hence, and have set up a war-temple on the radioactive cinder once known as Earth. As invasion looms, they have deployed a weapons platform known as the godmachine — but it requires a crew. With no pilots of their own, the Krax are recruiting from the deepest reaches of the past, and have misidentified Tesco as an order of cyborg battle monks. Before Tess can correct them, her superstore has been merged with the godmachine, and her team is stranded six billion years from Christmas. The gameplay that follows alternates between RPG and RTS segments: the former has Tess wander the bowels of the godmachine, tending to her staff and trying to learn more about the arcane behemoth. The latter pits the godmachine against city-sized beasts, huge starships and legions of techno-ghosts as it stands proudly over a holographic supermarket. As Tess marshals her colleagues and unravels mysteries in the RPG sections, she unlocks new powers for the battle segments: in time, giant brooms sprout from the godmachine's hull to sweep away infantry, while infrared laser turrets mimic the action of checkout scan guns. In the late game, Tess must choose between getting her staff back in time for Christmas, and sacrificing them for the Krax's war — after long enough in the captain's throne, she begins to forget which reality she started in. Ultimately, only her plucky crew can help her remember her humanity.

VERDICT

Incredibly challenging in its RTS segments, deeply written in its RPG portions, and dazzlingly beautiful throughout, *ELH* was a bold sponsorship move by Tesco — but a bloody successful one nonetheless.

"GIANT BROOMS SPROUT FROM THE GODMACHINE'S HULL TO SWEEP AWAY INFANTRY, WHILE INFRARED LASER TURRETS MIMIC THE ACTION OF CHECKOUT SCAN GUNS."

54 REALMS OF FIGHTINGE

MMO THAT JUST
WON'T DIE, DESPITE
GROTESQUELY
OVERPOWERED
SQUIDMEN,
APATHETIC DRAGONS
AND A SCANDAL
INVOLVING A DIGITAL
SQUATTER.

YEAR
2004

GENRE
Generic Fantasy / MMO

DEVELOPER
Hailstorm Entertainment

FORMAT
PC P4 3.8

When Hailstorm Entertainment launched *Realms of Fightinge* in 2004, it was just the latest game in the craze for massively multiplayer fantasy RPGs. Players could choose to play the elves or catpeople of the League, or the orcs and skeletons of the villainous Torrent – either way, play boiled down to fetching animal bums for unlovable NPCs in order to grind XP. Despite this, something about the game's lore, borrowed from Hailstorm's *Fightinge* series of RTS games, captured hearts worldwide and made the game virtually synonymous with its genre. But while *RoF* outlived its competitors, by the mid 2010s it was looking shabby, and haemorrhaging players. To stop the rot, Hailstorm drafted in marketing genius Mark Best (see *Ricky Feathers*, p.62), and gave him carte blanche to reinvent the game. Unfortunately, Best was… well, past his best, and he oversaw disasters such as the *Rise of the Squidmen* expansion, which introduced a race of tentacle-faced brutes so horrendously overpowered that they had to be instantly nerfed to the point of unplayability. In the end, both the game's salvation and Best's downfall came about at the hands of a short order cook named Colin Colinson. By means still unknown to this day, Colinson managed to *upload his consciousness into RoF and squat there.* He didn't have any aim in mind – he was just trying to avoid paying rent in real life. Nevertheless, the sheer impossibility of his presence had people flocking to the game just to gawp. Given his own failure to revive *RoF*, Best was furious at this, and went to ridiculous, villain-in-a-cartoon lengths to force the digital tramp to move on. In the end, Best was hoisted by his own petard – after forcing his team to code in a gamebreaking rooster specifically to kill Colin, he managed to completely ruin the launch of *RoF's Throne of Malfallax* expansion, and give Colin the chance to become a worldwide hero by slaying the bird. Best is long gone, but Colinson seems to be going nowhere – and so neither is *RoF*.

VERDICT

While it's really odd that no research has been done into the fact an actual human lives in it, *Realms of Fightinge* has outlived its original purpose as a game and become a sort of timeless curiosity.

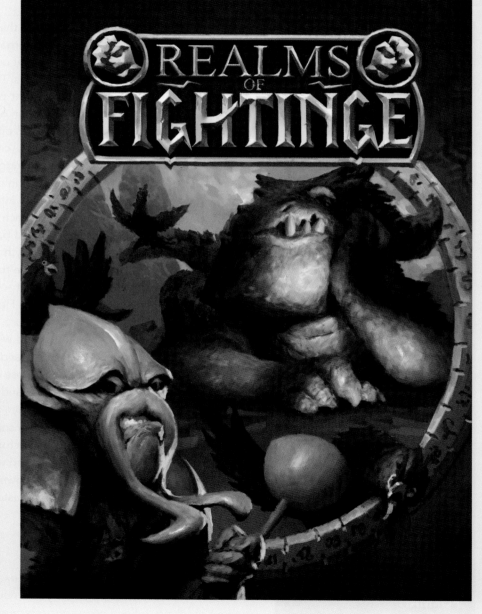

"PLAY BOILED DOWN TO FETCHING ANIMAL BUMS FOR UNLOVABLE NPCS IN ORDER TO GRIND XP."

55 TAKE ON ME BY A-HA: THE GAME

HARROWING, YET DISTURBINGLY STRAIGHTFORWARD, ADAPTATION OF THE FAMOUS MUSIC VIDEO.

YEAR
2004

GENRE
Hungry Ghosts / Racing / Rhythm

DEVELOPER
Rotoscope Rangers

FORMAT
PlayStation 2

This horror masterpiece tells the story of the demon Mort'en-H'kkt, as it fights to escape the pencil-sketch synthpop purgatory of Chiaroscuro and enter the Fleshrealm. Its first act is a racing game, set on a featureless plane where restless devils compete in endless motorcycle races. The contests are treacherous – lethal obstacles are often betrayed only by faint pencil marks, while corners can be drawn suddenly into existence at the whim of the game's engine. You start as a faint wisp of charcoal, but as you run others off the track you gain their substance, speed and inertia. Eventually, when you crackle with dark energy and pass through other motorcycles like mist, you trigger the game's next phase, in which you leer out of the pages of a shit comic in order to catch the eye of a human. Once you do so, you may extend a hand into the Fleshrealm and waggle until it is grasped. For every moment you breach the barrier your substance drains, and if you lose enough, you are banished back to the races. If you succeed in reeling a human in, however, a strange rhythm game begins in which the pair of you caper around a haunted mirror in time to the omnipresent beat. Follow the music closely enough and the spell is cast – you transfer some of your essence to the human, and gain an anchor in the Fleshrealm. But you must be quick – the presence of a human in the Chiaroscuro draws its ravenous inhabitants like moths to a flame, and they begin to arrive with hungry eyes and pipe wrenches in hand. At this point your human flees, and you must begin a series of brutal wrench duels in a claustrophobic maze. Lose and you are annihilated, but batter enough foes into smudges of grey gore and you may attempt the game's final feat – locating your human in the Fleshrealm and manifesting in meat-form. This process is physically painful, requiring ten solid minutes of button mashing and actual screaming (the game required a microphone) to complete. Nevertheless, if your stamina is up to it, you are rewarded with the game's final shot: Mort'en-H'kkt, drenched in sweat and slithering down a dim corridor, his face distending into a predatory smirk as he prepares to taste blood for the first time.

VERDICT

Sublimely horrible. While the game sticks exactly to the structure of the famous 1985 video, once you've played it you'll never be able to hear "Take on Me" without breaking out in anxious goosebumps.

"ESCAPE THE PENCIL-SKETCH SYNTHPOP PURGATORY OF CHIAROSCURO AND ENTER THE FLESHREALM."

FILM AND TV TIE-INS: PART ONE

While *Take on Me by A-ha: The Game* is notable as an adaptation that achieved vastly more in artistic terms than its originating work, the history of film-to-game adaptations is famously hit and miss. Here is a selection of the more interesting detritus left behind by thirty years of attempts to bring the silver screen to the thumbs of the masses:

01 MIDDLE AGED MUTANT NINJA TURTLES // Video Grahams, 1997

Melancholy 16-bit RPG where you must hold the turtles' lives together through health problems, failing marriages and the pressures of fatherhood. After Splinter's funeral the boys agree to hang out more, but their hearts aren't really in it – they just aren't the same people they were as teens. The game's final act, after Michelangelo dies young of heart failure, is unplayably sad.

02 GAWSH! // Digital Grandads, 2016

Indie jumpscare horror; an urban explorer breaks into an abandoned animation studio in search of priceless cels from an unreleased cartoon – too late, they realise they are being stalked by an emaciated dogman with peglike tusks and black ribbon ears, naked but for a green porkpie hat. By the time you hear the game's titular exclamation, it's always too late to run.

03 FLINTSTONES: UPRISING // Jollycom, 2003

Cel-shaded thriller that begins as a casual police procedural in the jaunty world of *The Flintstones*. Things get heavy quickly as Bedrock's megafauna, enslaved and used as comedic replacements for 1950s technology, rises in bloody revolt. As Fred Flintstone hollers while being eviscerated by a saber-toothed tiger, 'YABBA DABBA DON'T! PLEASE! NO! ARrrRGghh...'

04 SNAPE // Accio Entertainment, 2001

Potter-themed remake of the classic *Snake* phone game; Alan Rickman trudges round a dungeon, bollocking students. The more magical items he confiscates, the longer his robes get, and you must take care not to trip over them. In a saccharine nod to hyperfans, the Game Over screen simply bears the word "Always."

05 GARFIELD: MECHA DESTINY // Computer Swine, 2006

Bill Murray got surprisingly into voicing this inexplicable anime-styled adventure, in which Garfield pilots a giant, lasagna-fuelled cat mech in a desperate fight to eradicate the concept of Mondays forever. It's hard to blame him – considering that film-to-game adaptations are usually a pale reflection of their licenses, *Garfield: Mecha Destiny* was a baffling exception to the rule.

06 DRAINAGE! // Thunderswan Interactive, 2007

Frenetic puzzler licensed on *There Will Be Blood*; play as Daniel Day Lewis, sampling other peoples' milkshakes with a comically long straw. Drink enough milkshakes and you activate a minigame about beating a man to death in a bowling alley. Thunderswan were well known for being fans of DDL, having also produced an adaptation of *Gangs of New York* for the GameCube.

07 BEAST'S ANXIOUS DRINK // Two Arbitrary Words Studios, 2014

Troubling avant-garde exploration of *Beauty and the Beast* for Apple and Android devices; largely consists of relentless quicktime events in which you force Beast to anxiously chug cans of soft drink while he stares straight into the camera. Nothing has ever looked so worried as Beast trying to drink a can of cherry coke in three seconds.

08 GRAND THEFT AUTOBOTS // Rancid Principle Software, 2008

Surprisingly good take on the dire *Transformers* franchise; play as a high-tech thief who prowls a city by night, trying to identify cars which can turn into robots, before duelling and enslaving them to sell for big bucks. Gets a bit disturbing when you attempt to force-transform cars which are currently being driven by humans.

09 MURPHY'S LAW // Pickled Egg Games, 2001

Legal procedural sequel to the *Robocop* trilogy, in which half-mechanical lawman Alex Murphy, following a renunciation of violence, takes the bar in order to pursue justice in the Detroit court system. Features ED-209 as a defence attorney, wearing an incredibly ill-fitting suit as it defends a series of futuristic lowlives.

10 JURASSIC PARK ACCOUNTANT // Dogsoft, 1993

In this spreadsheet-heavy PC title, it's your job to manage John Hammond's increasingly intricate tax situation as his dinosaur theme park goes to shit. Let's just get this out of the way now – you never see a single bloody dinosaur in this game, although good grief do you learn a lot about their capital gains implications.

2005 TO 2010

56 THOMAS THE WAR ENGINE

PLAY AS AN APOCALYPTIC WAR MACHINE, CRAFTED FROM THE BONES OF A HERO AND THE WRECK OF A BOY-FACED TRAIN, AS IT FIGHTS FOR HOPE IN A SHATTERED WORLD.

YEAR
2005

GENRE
Enchanted Trains / Epic RPG

DEVELOPER
The Venison Parallax

FORMAT
Xbox 360

It is the year 2560, and Earth is recovering from a cataclysmic war between man and train. The land is still blackened by coal dust from the Chuggening, but plants are finally poking through the rails that encrust the continents, and humanity is rising from the ashes of the locomotocene. But this brittle hope is threatened by the ambitions of a madman: a warlord calling himself the Fat Controller has led his forces to the forbidden Isle of Sodor, where he has cracked the concrete sarcophagus of the Traingrave. Day and night, his citadel booms with industry, as metal serpents are winched from the earth, and cold boilers are coaxed to life by the sacrifice of slave battalions. As the mournful whistles of the trains sound once again over the land, the shaman-queens form a desperate council. After long debate, a terrible conclusion is reached – to fight trains, they must use trains themselves. From deep beneath their holy mountain, a wreck is recovered – Thomas, the arch-train – along with the bones of Awdry, the hero who slew it. For ten days, blacksmiths labour to forge a titan from the wreck – a train in the shape of a man, with a hero's bones at its core. The beast is awoken with a handful of sacred coal, and swears fealty to the queendom. So begins *Thomas the War Engine*. Narrated by Ringo Starr doing his best post-apocalyptic growl, the game followed Thomas in his quest to hunt down the undead trains of the Fat Controller across a savagely beautiful post-industrial wilderness. Boss fights could happen at any time, and were breathtaking; the trains seemed genuinely bestial, clanking and hissing as they thundered over the railscape, flanks bristling with harpoon-wielding cultists. After a half-hour duel with one of these leviathans, the thrill of executing a finishing move with Thomas's sword, Boiler-Piercer, was visceral. The writing was no less powerful: while Thomas is thoroughly heroic, he is shunned as an abomination by his people – a monster made necessary by dire circumstance. When children pelt him with old bolts on the outskirts of a village he has just saved from a mob of coal trucks, you really feel the tears of oil he weeps.

VERDICT

An undisputed blockbuster, this Xbox 360 launch title not only set the bar for seventh generation console gaming – it redefined the open world RPG. Choo fucking *choo*.

"HUNT DOWN THE UNDEAD TRAINS OF THE FAT CONTROLLER ACROSS A SAVAGELY BEAUTIFUL POST-INDUSTRIAL WILDERNESS."

57 HAWKS VS. VOLES ONLINE

DISASTROUSLY ONE-SIDED MMO

YEAR
2005

GENRE
Nature / MMO

DEVELOPER
Red Flag Games

FORMAT
PC Pentium D 2.8, Athlon 64 X2 3600+

While in recent years games designers have become excited by the concept of asymmetry in competitive games (*They Think It's All Ogres, Duckhorse Cataclysm, Ultra Drug Olympics*), it's never quite been handled like it was in *Hawks vs. Voles Online*. There was a brutal simplicity to it all: new players were assigned a faction at random, with one in a thousand getting to be a hawk, and the rest getting lumbered with voles. And in the first year of the game's existence, things went exactly as you might imagine – the virtual meadow in which the game took place was an arena of terror, with voles falling by the thousand to the beaks of diving hawks. But then everything changed. Somewhere in the depths of a forum, a shadowy cabal of *HVVO* aficionados assembled to figure out how to swing things in the voles' favour. By wringing every possible exploit from the game's commendably complex physics engine, and executing perfect teamwork across thousands of players, they theorised it would be possible for the rodent side to take down a single hawk before being wiped. And so, on June 20th, 2006, the impossible happened: taking orders from a massive IRC command room, 6,450 vole players worked to the same plan, and beat the shit out of a hawk when it swooped. The community was in uproar, and when the dust settled, they noticed something astonishing: when the hawk died, all of the other hawks *became infinitesimally weaker*. It turns out this was *a feature of the game*. Smelling blood, the cabal organised another attack, and scored another kill. Again, the hawks became weaker, and things escalated further. By the time the hawk faction had even begun to talk about co-ordinating their own efforts, the scales had tipped, and hawks were going down by the dozen. By 2007 the game was abandoned – because it was no longer viable to play as a hawk. The experiment had been successful.

Standard vole character classes in *Hawks vs Voles Online*:

Scurrier: Basic vole. Goes down like a sack of shit if a hawk gets anywhere near it.

Fat vole: Has two hit points rather than the single hit point of most voles, but moves at half speed.

Vole paladin: Can save one other vole from death by leaping into the beak of a hawk in its place.

Vole mage: Can cast Rancidity, giving voles a one in five chance to cause indigestion in hawks.

Gun vole: Has a tiny gun with a single bullet, which can take 1 hit point off a hawk if the wind is behind it.

VERDICT

A shit MMO admittedly, but a cracking sociopolitical experiment nonetheless.

"6,450 VOLE PLAYERS WORKED TO THE SAME PLAN, AND BEAT THE SHIT OUT OF A HAWK WHEN IT SWOOPED."

58 SHADOW OF THE PUB MAN

MELANCHOLY ART GAME COMPRISING A SERIES OF BOSS FIGHTS THAT ENGENDER DEEP FEELINGS OF LONELINESS AND SORROW.

YEAR
2005

GENRE
Nihilism / Action

DEVELOPER
Goosepipes: Re-Ducks

FORMAT
PlayStation 2

Shadow of the Pub Man took one of the most overused themes in gaming – cockney pub violence – and wrought it into something profound. While many other games in this book have involved rough men battering each other to death in manky alcohol dungeons, this one merely used that as a familiar canvas on which to explore themes of empathy, death and futility. The premise was very simple – a young man must seek out sixteen Pub Men in a crumbling city, and cancel their lives. It's never exactly clear why the protagonist is doing this, but it's implied that if he succeeds he will bring his girlfriend back to life, or something. The Pub Men can be located by taking a puff on a cigarette, and seeing which way the wind blows the smoke. You are aided by a dented bicycle which you can summon by shouting "oi, wanker" at the top of your lungs, but even on two wheels, it takes ages to traverse the game's world. And what a world. Perhaps the most striking aspect of *Shadow* is how desolate it is – other than you and the Pub Men themselves, the city you wander is almost entirely lifeless. Occasionally a fox will cross a street in the distance, but other than that it's just you and the wind. Of course, the game is anything but dull – once you find the Pub Men, it's white knuckle combat all the way. But even during pitched fighting, the sense of melancholy remains. Each battle in the game has a similar structure – a bruiser will stagger out of his pub into the car park, point at you while roaring the c-word, then put down his pint and charge. What happens next can vary with the environment – one fight involves drowning a Pub Man in a carrier bag-choked pond, while another involves tricking a lion-faced bastard into repeatedly crashing through scaffolding. In the end, though, each fight ends the same – as the Pub Man in question dies, the lager in his glass begins to snake through the air towards your mouth, and no matter how fast you run, you can't escape drinking it. When you kill the last Pub Man and finish the sixteenth pint, the screen fades to black, and there is a long pause. When vision returns, you have changed, with a ghastly sense of inevitability, into one of the Pub Men.

VERDICT

Even now, *Shadow of the Pub Man* remains at the vanguard of the debate over whether games can be art, and for good reason – it was deep and murky as the heart of a Pub Man.

"ONCE YOU FIND THE PUB MEN, IT'S WHITE KNUCKLE COMBAT ALL THE WAY."

59 SILENT BUTCHER

STEALTH GAME WHERE YOU PLAY A HUGE, RUDDY-FACED MAN TRYING TO PREPARE JOINTS OF MEAT WITHOUT WAKING HIS TWELVE ANGRY SONS.

YEAR
2006

GENRE
Butchery / Survival Horror

DEVELOPER
Partyboy Studios

FORMAT
Nintendo Wii

As pioneering as *Silent Butcher* was in its use of motion-sensitive controls, it was something of a commercial blunder. When Nintendo agreed to it as a third party launch title for the family-friendly Wii, they were expecting the game they had been pitched by Partyboy Studios – a pastel-coloured tale about a cartoon butcher, who had to chop meat without disturbing the sleep of his dopey, apple-headed son. This would have been the game they received, if Partyboy's entire art team hadn't been busted for running an illegal dog fighting operation just three weeks into production. Attempting to style out the disaster, Partyboy's directors handed over production to a whole new team, and the change of aesthetic was… dark. Using your controller as a cleaver, you played a bruise-ridden butcher, working by night to prepare unidentifiable carcasses for sale the next day. The catch was that you had to do so as quietly as possible – every thud too loud, each clatter of dropped steel or crumpling of a beer can underfoot, risked waking one of the butcher's Twelve Angry Sons. It's impossible to forget your first encounter with one of the Sons – skittering towards you, eyes glazed over with blank hatred, they could only be quelled by tossing them fresh meat, which would in turn deplete your stock for the day's trading. And the less meat you sold, the less you had to spend on soundproofing for the next night's work. Some of the Sons, like light-sleeping Gustav, were easy to avoid – his roaring made it relatively easy to hear him coming in time to hide. But when you encountered Heinrich, an emaciated titan who would only awake to the sound of bleeding, things got terrifying. There's no doubt *Silent Butcher* was a buggy release – gyroscope issues meant you quite often ended up slamming your cleaver into the low ceiling when you meant to quietly set it down, while clipping issues with the Sons mean they would occasionally reach through walls – but these moments only added to the game's sense of ever-escalating panic.

VERDICT

To this day, an entire generation can't help but feel slightly on edge when making a sandwich at night, and so *Silent Butcher* can be fairly called a classic despite modest sales.

"GYROSCOPE ISSUES MEANT YOU QUITE OFTEN ENDED UP SLAMMING YOUR CLEAVER INTO THE LOW CEILING WHEN YOU MEANT TO QUIETLY SET IT DOWN."

60 QUADBIKE SORCERER

OPEN WORLD EXTREME SPORTS FANTASY; ROAM THE LAND AS A MIGHTY WIZARD ASTRIDE A MYSTICAL ATV, RIGHTING WRONGS WITH SPELLS AND STUNTS ALIKE.

YEAR
2006

GENRE
High Fantasy / Extreme Sports

DEVELOPER
Mithrandir Developments

FORMAT
PlayStation 3

A forest canopy at the height of summer; birdsong and the lazy drone of bees. A breeze rustles the leaves, and we hear distant shouts. Cut to: a man in mud-stained travelling clothes, bound with grubby rope, struggles on a dirt track. We pan up; sat on a barrel of wine, a leering goblin brandishes a rusty dagger in its claws. The wicked creature chuckles and helps itself to another cup of wine; beside the road, its fellows rifle through the merchant's overturned cart. It is a scene of callous injustice, and the goblin chief is clearly relishing his victim's dismay. But then something changes on the creature's face; as the humming of the bees grows louder in the distance, fear crystallises. The hum builds to a growl, and the heads of the other goblins snap up from their looting. This is not the sound of bees. A parallax zoom leaves the goblins in the foreground, and we focus on a rise in the forest track. Beyond it, the noise builds – it is a throaty roar now, with something else underlying it. A human voice, bellowing an incantation. The goblins turn to flee, but it is too late: their reckoning is upon them. A chorus of voices blasts out in song as we glance back at the road; in slow motion, a blazing shape crests the rise and hangs in the air like a breaching dolphin. It is a flame-red ATV, sun glinting from immaculate chrome fittings, and it's ridden by a wizard in flowing cerulean robes. His face is cast in righteous fury, his hair whips in the wind of his passage. Around his bone-white staff, fire coils in a tight spiral. With a shout of command, he levels the staff at the goblins, and flames surge forth. The screen fades to black with a WHOOMPH of fire, and the main refrain from "Journey of the Sorcerer" by the Eagles plays slowly on the plucked strings of a dulcimer. That's the opening cinematic from *Quadbike Sorcerer*, and if that alone doesn't earn it a place as one of the most remarkable games of all time, then we're not sure what will.

VERDICT

It's about a wizard, who rides a magical quadbike. Come on. What more do you need to know?

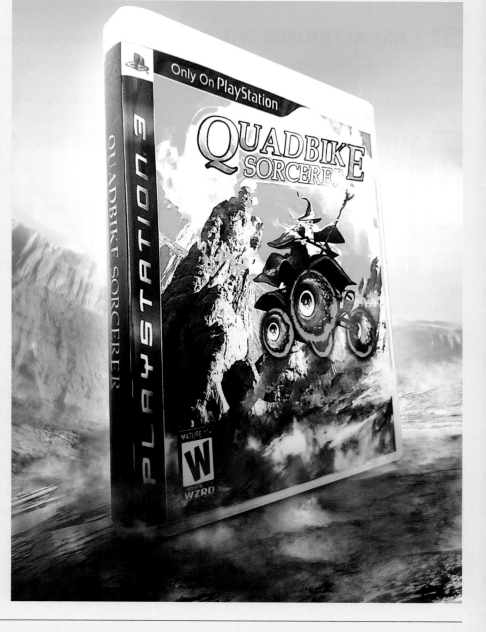

"THE MAIN REFRAIN FROM JOURNEY OF THE SORCERER BY THE EAGLES PLAYS SLOWLY ON THE PLUCKED STRINGS OF A DULCIMER."

FILM AND TV TIE-INS: PART TWO

Presuming you've recovered from *Quadbike Sorcerer*, here are ten more classic games adapted from the world of the moving image:

01 I AM ALTERING THE DAHL // Hard Times Productions, 2016

Hypertense choice-based RPG where you must survive ordering, eating and paying for a curry for two with Darth Vader. Features a famously heart-stopping set-piece where, in an attempt to pass the dark lord his pilau rice, you accidentally knock his beer and get it all over the samosas. Tip: do not even think about discussing splitting the bill.

02 SUPER DEADWOOD // Free Gratis Games, 2005

Play as Seth, Sol or Alma in this frenetic 8-bit platformer based on the ultraviolent TV masterpiece. Collect gold nuggets while avoiding the barrels thrown by Al Swearengen from the balcony of his saloon. Contains a grim bonus stage in which traumatised civil war doctor Amos Cochran attempts to treat an entire brothel full of venereal diseases with limited supplies.

03 REAL STEEL: THE MEAL OF EELS // Grubio, 2011

Weird spin-off of the robot boxing film in which you play as Hugh Jackman, attempting to wolf down a bathtub full of live eels quicker than a series of robot opponents. It's a mediocre game, made brilliant by Jackman's candidly exasperated voice acting – lines like "why are we eating these eels?" and "robots don't even like eels" really speak to the enigma at the game's heart.

04 IRON MAN: DRUNK AT THE WHEEL // Badgerbreath Studios, 2009

This uncompromising flight sim veers wildly away from the Marvel Cinematic Universe's light touch when it comes to Tony Stark's drinking problem, and portrays the terrifying reality of being pissed in a near-invincible suit of flying armour. The only problem with the game is, despite its incredibly serious social message, it's really, really fun to play.

05 DANCE DANCE PACIFIC RIM // Bloated Crow, 2013

Two-player co-op game for Xbox Kinect, simulating the experience of piloting one of the movie's skyscraper-sized fight machines: each player must stride and punch in near perfect synchronicity, according to instructions flashing on screen, in order to make the magic happen. The closer the actions of the two players, the more powerful the rocket-driven punches that result.

06 SUPER ENEMY AT THE GATES // Spectacular Blunders, 2001

Harrowing scenes from the battle of Stalingrad, interpreted via wildly inappropriate cartoon graphics and colourful arcade fun. Action alternates between side-scrolling infantry sequences (Crossing the Volga! Charges into machine gun fire!), and first-person sniping rounds played using a light gun peripheral. Toweringly disrespectful, but – unfortunately – a proper laugh.

07 PLANET EARTH II: THE GAME // Fast Owl Entertainment, 2016

Retro 16 bit-style platformer based on the landmark BBC wildlife series. Levels include: monkeys stealing fruit while scampering over city rooftops, swimming between islands as a sloth, lions versus giraffes, and a final 'iguanas chased by snakes' level that is honestly almost too stressful to contemplate, let alone play.

08 SCOOBY DOO AND THE 100 YEARS' WAR // Tellykings, 2015

Point-and-click adventure where the gang are transported to 15th-century France and must survive a hell of mud, blood, hooves and steel. There are no ghosts, and no mysteries to solve: just whistling arrows, burning farms, and huge armoured men with bloodshot eyes and no emotions left except for hate. There is a great bit where Shaggy and Scooby make a very tall sandwich, though.

09 CORPORATE LAWYERS OF DUNE // Digital Champions, 1984

This incredibly sober film tie-in from Digital Champions gave sci-fi fans the treat they had always dreamed of: navigating the baroque tax regulations of the *Dune* Universe in order to optimise House Atreides' balance sheet. Not a game worth knowing about, other than to have an answer to the question "was any game more boring than *Jurassic Park Accountant*?" (p. 141).

10 THE SCORPION KING 2: RISE OF A WARRIOR: THE BOOK: THE GAME // Rushjob Studios, 2008

Perhaps due to some rule of double negatives, or just by sheer, melon-bollocked pluck, this game adaptation of a novelisation of the sequel to a spinoff of a remake of an old horror film ended up being a full-on orgasm of a game. Despite being six degrees of separation from an intellectual property that made sense, it was smartly written, beautifully designed, and spawned a multiplayer community that not only remains active to this day, but is the basis of a televised sport in South Korea.

61 WASP GETTER 6

THE CROWN JEWEL IN A SERIES THAT BROUGHT THE FUN OF WASP-GETTING TO MILLIONS OF HOMES.

YEAR
2006

GENRE
Wasps / Getting

DEVELOPER
Chimpsong

FORMAT
PC Pentium D 3.73

Although it may be tempting fate to say this with the release of *Wasp Getter: Generations* just around the corner, this game was where the *Wasp Getter* franchise peaked. Fans may speak highly of other instalments, but few would disagree this was the one that got it all right – the graphics were perfectly pitched between whimsy and realism, the sound design was unnervingly strong, and gameplay allowed for endless replayability without things getting stale. And let's not forget, this game had its work cut out for it – 2005's *Wasp Getter 5* had been an immense disappointment, amounting to little more than a re-skin of *WG4* with a new orchard map, and fans were hacked off. Many had cynically dismissed the series as a cash cow for developer Chimpsong, and took the hype around *WG6* with a pinch of salt. When the first reviews came in, however, they changed their tune. The game had somehow managed to reinvent Wasp Getting, while retaining Stingzone, the Stripy Café, and other fan favourites. The familiar eight categories of wasp were all back (the models looked perfect even in Hornet Mode), and bees were finally gettable, having been famously dropped from *WG4* during development. What's more, the crisp satisfaction of the new 'Turbo Get' mechanic had to be experienced to be believed. Of course, *WG6* wasn't perfect: the game struggled online, as simultaneous Team Gets fell foul of lag issues, and Bee Gets outside of campaign mode had major stability problems. Nevertheless, *Wasp Getter* was always a game best played solo, and so these issues had little impact on reviews.

The press on *Wasp Getter 6*:

"You'll find yourself picking up the phone and exclaiming 'Dad, I got a wasp' to people who aren't even your dad. I cried most days." – Jimmy Blunce, *PC Warlord*

"While I'd never be able to get wasps in real life, I no longer feel I need to. This game has, without doubt, shown me how it must feel." – Michael Stabbener, *Games Prophet*

"I swear on my mother's life, I got those wasps so hard their fucking ancestors felt it. Bring me another wasp, I feel like a god." – Ted Reckless, *Financial Times*

VERDICT

Innovative, beautiful, and expertly polished, *WG6* is a game that, despite three of its sequels earning Game of the Year status, is yet to be improved on. As the marketing campaign around its release had it, "you'd best believe the buzz."

"THE CRISP SATISFACTION OF THE NEW 'TURBO GET' MECHANIC HAD TO BE EXPERIENCED TO BE BELIEVED."

62 ASTROHOUND BOMBARDIER

STRANGELY
DESOLATE PHYSICS
PUZZLER WHERE
YOU USE A PARTICLE
ACCELERATOR
TO FIRE DOGS AT
DISTANT OBJECTS IN
SPACE.

YEAR
2007

GENRE
Astrophysics / Puzzler

DEVELOPER
Grozart Labs

FORMAT
PlayStation Portable

Space is a forbidding place. Having spent our entire evolutionary history in the embrace of a gravity well, cushioned under a duvet of warm air, it is a realm we are barely fit to comprehend, let alone conquer. *Astrohound Bombardier* was a stark reminder of this terrible truth. You wouldn't think it, given the game's cartoony box art and comedy premise, but it was an intrinsically chilly experience. Things got disconcerting from the moment you switched the game on, with its 'unique' control scheme requiring the PlayStation Portable to be turned sideways in order to play. Some players claimed this was pretty satisfying if you had the thumbs for the job, but this was clearly bollocks. Unless your thumbs were prehensile meat ropes, the game was utter hell to control, and it was meant to be that way. Then there was the sound design. Echoing, plinky-plonk noises that might have been part of a composition, or might have been randomly generated, interspersed occasionally with the tinny, desperately faint sound of astronauts going mad. And to cap it all off, the haunting whine of the dogs as you loaded them into the particle accelerator. That was when it hit you – this wasn't a funny premise at all. You were firing dogs into fucking *space*. And not even for any good reason – just because a game was telling you to. They were going to die out there, like bloody Laika. But you persevered, because you wanted to get a high score. More fool you, because that's when the maths started. After the first few practice shots, the game began asking you to calculate and input truly ghastly bits of physics in order to make a shot. "Given the desired launch velocity and angle, please solve for the coefficients of the quadratic specifying the closest fit to the resulting trajectory," the game would say in a dispassionate monotone, and then wait until you either got a degree or gave up. Even if you called up a genius to get the answer, things barely got easier – while the dogs being fired would quickly accelerate to appreciable fractions of the speed of light, the game would still model their flight in real time. It wasn't uncommon to learn the result of a shot hours or even days after it had been fired. The lesson learned from all this? Space is bigger than you, space is smarter than you, and space hates you. It is not a laughing matter.

VERDICT

Don't muck around with space.

"AFTER THE FIRST FEW PRACTICE SHOTS, THE GAME BEGAN ASKING YOU TO CALCULATE AND INPUT TRULY GHASTLY BITS OF PHYSICS IN ORDER TO MAKE A SHOT."

63 BREAD EGG REDEMPTION

OPEN WORLD WESTERN WHERE EVERY CHARACTER YOU ENCOUNTER IS INEXPLICABLY OBSESSED WITH EGGS ON TOAST.

YEAR
2007

GENRE
Eggs / Western / RPG

DEVELOPER
Smashboy North

FORMAT
PlayStation 3

When it first appeared on shelves, most Western gamers assumed that *Bread Egg Redemption* was one of those games whose title had lost something in translation. On first glance, it looked to be a fairly straight-laced cowboy-themed RPG, with a name that had probably been an elegant play on words in Japanese, but which had been mangled on its trip across the world. After all, the history of games is littered with titles whose names suffered from being rammed into English – just look at other 2007 releases such as *Steel Burglar Purgatory*, *Beef Animal Country Boy*, and *Grandpa Reign: Deadly Spookalikes*. But there was one problem with this hypothesis. *Bread Egg Redemption* had been programmed in Leeds, and named precisely for what it was: a game about cowboys who fucking love eggs. Of course, this was an issue that had been raised early in development, as its publisher had become nervous about how the market would react to a triple-A title so resolutely themed around hen fruit. But lead developer Tommy Plums stuck to his course, like a grim-faced sea captain steering his ship straight into a rocky shoreline, and the game was completed according to his grand design. The result was surprisingly engaging: once you got past the relentless egg-boiling segments and the bread-toasting minigames, the game served up a raw, sweat-and-leather vision of a frontier populated by swindlers, outlaws, and bounty hunters with hearts of gold. It just happened to serve it up with a heavy side of eggs. The gunfights in the game, for example, were electrifying, with a brilliant control mechanic that evoked the finger-twitching tension of standoffs from the silver screen. But before you could duel an opponent, they would insist you sit down and join them for a 15-egg cookout under the blazing noon sun. This was frustrating, to say the least. Nevertheless, for all its sins, the game gave players an encyclopaedic knowledge of how to prepare eggs, and that's never a bad thing.

VERDICT

Playing *Bread Egg Redemption*, one couldn't help but feel one was in the presence of a once-in-a-generation masterpiece, hidden behind a maddening layer of egg chat.

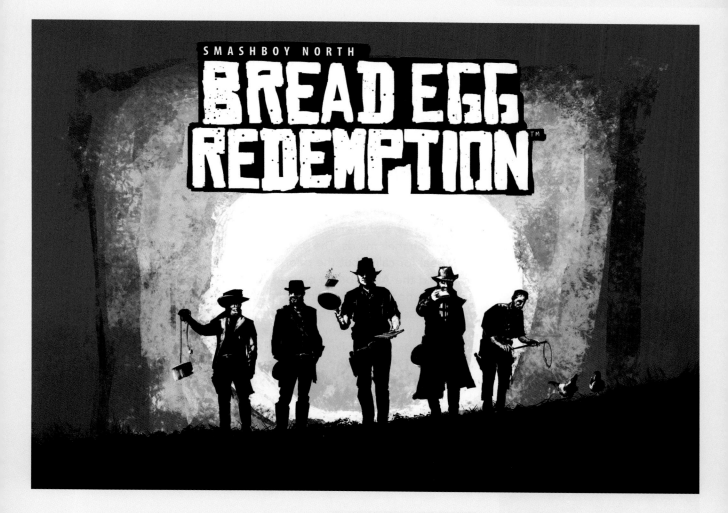

"BEFORE YOU COULD DUEL AN OPPONENT, THEY WOULD INSIST YOU SIT DOWN AND JOIN THEM FOR A 15-EGG COOKOUT UNDER THE BLAZING NOON SUN."

64 GET DOWN, MR PRESIDENT!

PROTECT DISCOVIA'S PRESIDENT BY USING SWEET MOVES TO FOIL ASSASSINATION ATTEMPTS.

YEAR
2007

GENRE
Oppression / Dance

DEVELOPER
Magnamunch Systems

FORMAT
PlayStation 3

The year is 2007. But in the People's Funkocratic Republic of Discovia, you wouldn't know it. In this locked-down dictatorship, somewhere vaguely in the Balkans, all calendars were burned in 1977, and the state transitioned to Party Time forever. Factories were nationalised to produce flares, sequins and oversized sunglasses, and all public spaces were bulldozed to make way for sprawling discotheques. Each day begins with families dancing in formation before a disco ball engraved with the president's face, and the nation subsists on tiny, dry pellets known as Disco Biscuits. It is a living nightmare, and the populace has been on the edge of riot for decades, only quelled by the exhaustion inflicted by constant, state-mandated move-busting. Today, they have been pushed over the edge. The president's announcement of a one-thousand-day celebration of Boney M has sparked a protest that has grown out of control, and the citizenry have marched on the presidential palace with violence on their minds. The president has taken to the steps of his residence to appeal for calm, but the people aren't having any of it. They're ready to snap, and the Abba being blasted on loop really isn't calming them down. As one of the president's elite cadre of bodyguards, it's your job to watch for potential assassins, and protect the father of the state by any means possible. There's only one problem: he has decreed that you must not, at any point, stop disco dancing while doing so. The result is a frenetic, beat-driven beat-'em-up in which constant vigilance and fluid hip movements are all that stand between you and disaster. You must protect the president on the palace steps, then through the opulent halls within as protesters overrun the grounds, and finally on his helicopter pad, which is of course floored with flashing, coloured panels. In a climactic final encounter, a group of rebels have managed to jack into the state speaker system, and are intermittently changing the music to classic rock – if you want to keep the president alive until the helicopter lifts off, you'll just have to find a way to keep disco alive too.

VERDICT

Although its casual stereotyping of southeastern European states as mad dictatorships probably isn't okay, it's hard not to warm to Discovia's strutting lunacy – by the end of the game, you find yourself genuinely caring not just about the president's survival, but about disco itself.

"FRENETIC, BEAT-DRIVEN BEAT-'EM-UP IN WHICH
CONSTANT VIGILANCE AND FLUID HIP MOVEMENTS
ARE ALL THAT STAND BETWEEN YOU AND DISASTER."

65 VIN DIESEL'S WEASEL EASEL

TRANSCENDENTALLY RELAXING ART GAME; PAINT ALONG WITH VIN'S INSTRUCTIONS TO CREATE DELIGHTFUL SMALL MAMMAL PORTRAITS.

YEAR
2008

GENRE
Weasels / Art

DEVELOPER
Platypus Games

FORMAT
PC Core 2 Duo 2.13,
Nintendo DS

Sometimes, when the world gets too much and you wonder how you're going to make it through the week, you just need a strong man to take care of you and teach you how to paint weasels. Frankly, it's amazing it took humanity until 2008 to create this game, which blended simple paint-by-numbers gameplay with innovative FMV techniques in order to perfectly simulate the experience of painting small carnivores with Vin Diesel. Encouraged by the reassuring croak of Diesel's voice, and guided by intuitive visual instructions, even the most stolidly uncreative person could find themselves painting beautiful images of weasels at play within hours. Particularly accurate brushwork would earn praise from Vin, while engaging in lengthy stints of colouring would see him put down his paintbrush to let you catch up, while offering short anecdotes from his acting career. Indeed, the game's Nintendo DS port built the rapport even further, with Diesel's face appearing on the console's upper screen as you painted on the lower, nodding and smiling at your progress like a watchful tutor. It was truly charming stuff, and part of the game's joy was in how much Vin was clearly enjoying taking part. Of course, this wasn't the action star's first outing into video games – 2005 had seen him star in *The Vast and the Curious*, a mystery game in which he voiced the internal monologue of a blue whale as it explored a tranquil alien sea. But not only did *Weasel Easel* allow him to continue exploring his tremendously sensitive inner self – it also finally allowed him to share his love of painting weasels with the world. All this isn't to say it was a perfect game, however: it certainly had its limitations. For experienced artists, or those after a challenge, the pace could be frustratingly slow – although some might argue that such players just needed to learn to relax more. Perhaps harder to argue with was the observation that the game's focus on weasels was a little restrictive. And while this was addressed by developer Platypus Games in their release of *Sean Bean's Scenes with Wolverines* the following year, it didn't escape critics' attention that the game had not moved away from the Mustelidae family of mammals, to which both weasels and wolverines obviously belong.

VERDICT

If you like Vin Diesel, and you're into weasels, this game'll infect your soul like measles.

Level 11: "Triple Leks"

3 more paintings until
level 12: "Fast and Furryous"

New Species Unlocked!
Mustela nigripes - 5 / 28 paintings

New Paintings Available!
Mustela putorius - 2 new scenes

"EVEN THE MOST STOLIDLY UNCREATIVE PERSON COULD FIND THEMSELVES PAINTING BEAUTIFUL IMAGES OF WEASELS AT PLAY WITHIN HOURS."

CELEBRITY TIE-INS

Vin Diesel's Weasel Easel was a standout hit both for its gameplay concept and for the enthusiasm with which A-lister Diesel approached the project. Yet while it is regarded as an apex of quality in the history of celebrity tie-ins, it is by no means in sparse company. Here are some other noteworthy titles which have shot to fame on the back of big names:

01 MIKE MYERS' MIRE OF WIRES // Osmium Box Games, 2016

Frantic VR puzzler featuring the voice of Canadian comedian Mike Myers, talking you through a series of increasingly tense and complex bomb defusal situations. Levels are themed on Myers' films – the tutorial features local access TV star Wayne Campbell, while later levels feature insufferable buck-toothed spy Austin Powers, and Shrek, who for some reason now lives in Iraq.

02 RU PAUL'S BAG RACE // Unknown, 2014

A work of rogue genius, Ru Paul's Bag Race was a piece of malware uploaded to thousands of self-serve supermarket checkouts during the summer of 2014; infected machines would seem possessed by the legendary TV glamazon, cajoling you to pack faster than other shoppers while making snide but harmless guesswork comments about your fashion sense.

03 GEORGE FOREMAN'S NORMAN LAWMEN // BrutusArts, 1994

A magic grilling machine sends retired boxer George Foreman back to eleventh century England, where he must solve crimes with a posse of armoured knights. While this quirky point-and-click adventure was released to promote the George Foreman grill, legal action soon forced its makers to issue a statement clarifying that it did not in fact possess the power of time travel.

04 NOEL'S HOUSE ARREST // Unknown, 2000

A year after the BBC cancelled Saturday night landmark *Noel's House Party*, this mysterious horror game appeared for free online. Having awoken in a prison cell deep under Noel Edmonds' boarded-up mansion, players had to escape and flee the deserted village of Crinkley Bottom without encountering its sole remaining resident, Blobby. The supposedly lovable pink figure had taken on an emaciated, ghoulish aspect: without warning he would come racing out of the dark on all fours like a beast, his eyes spinning and his tombstone teeth caked with gore.

05 JIMMY NAIL'S 'A TALE OF WHALES' // King Crab Software, 1998

Narrative adventure, in which players captain a Victorian whaling ship whose crew members are all voiced by

Geordie actor and musician Jimmy Nail. Although the occasional musical interludes were a little jarring – instead of sea shanties, the crew would occasionally burst into a rousing rendition of "Crocodile Shoes" – this was a surprisingly thrilling and historically accurate little title.

06 THE ROCK & A HARD PLACE // Brahma Bull Studios, 2015

This blockbuster caper redefined what action games could do with destructible terrain. Featuring actual demigod Dwayne 'The Rock' Johnson, it began with the ex-wrestler locked in a jail made from the hardest mineral on earth... the hardest, that is, except for the teeth of Dwayne 'The Rock' Johnson. The rest of the game, including Johnson's trademark one-liners, practically wrote itself.

07 MICKEY ROURKE'S BORKED ORCS: REDUX // Atomic Hyperworlds, 2017

The original *MRBO* was released in 1995, when Rourke's career was at a low and he would take pretty much any job that paid. The result was tragic – Mickey's image seemed tacked onto a game about a high fantasy hospital that had nothing to do with him, and his few hurried cutscene appearances seemed riven with contempt for the material he was working with. As such, it was a joy to see Rourke star in a high-budget VR remake of the game. In *MRBO: Redux*, the clearly reinvigorated actor played Thudgarr Sawbone, a heroic greenskin surgeon who talked the player through the mending of ruptured orcs on a fantasy battlefield. Rourke's gravel voice was perfect for the job, and it stands as one of the finest VR titles on the market at the time of going to print.

08 GREGG WALLACE'S SCRAPYARD BANQUET // Sad Alien Studios, 2011

Tablet game in which you control cultists searching a scrapyard for metal meals to quench the appetite of their god, Gregg Wallace. The *Masterchef* judge sits on a throne of burned out cars at the yard's heart, roaring for sustenance and devouring all you can bring him like a giant meat JCB.

09 MICHAEL STIPE'S HYPER PIPES // Single Cell Games, 2001

In this game produced by an experimental games division of Stipe's own production company, players must control the flight of the REM frontman as he hurtles through a web of psychedelic space tubes to a soundtrack of his band's greatest hits. It's fairly mega.

10 RAY MEARS' STRAY BEERS // Bushmeat Developments, 2008

TV survivalist Ray and his long suffering mate Gordon have mislaid nine tins of Heineken in the woods; can you find them all? This simple puzzle game for stoners is the sequel to the (barely interactive) *Ray Mears' Grey Fears*, in which Ray is out walking on a foggy night and must confront a series of his most frequent nightmares, including Fire Won't Start, Big Owl, Goblins, and Flammable Hands.

66 SPICEWORLD: LEGACY

FUTURISTIC RTS; LEGIONS OF CULTISTS FIGHT OVER THE RESOURCES OF A DISTANT WORLD, IN THE NAME OF FIVE IMMORTAL WARRIOR QUEENS.

YEAR
2008

GENRE
1990s Pop Music / RTS

DEVELOPER
Drastic Measures

FORMAT
Smartphone

"I'll tell you what I want, what I really really want. So tell me what you want, what you really want. I want absolute power. Ready the dropships." So begins *Spiceworld: Legacy*; in glossy pink letters against a background of deepest black. The text fades, a deep rumble shakes the screen, and a titanic spacecraft glides by overhead. The camera rises to show us its destination – a drab brown world, held in the roasting embrace of a dying red star. This is the planet Britpop-Omega-7, and it is about to become the galaxy's fiercest war zone, thanks to the vast deposits of precious spice recently discovered under its irradiated soil. Racing to orbit are five hypercarriers, each in service to one of the galaxy's five matriarchal houses, and each sworn to claim the world for their undying god-queen. The ships have been in flight for centuries; the women who launched them are long dead, succeeded by generations of parthenogenetic daughters who know nothing but the worship of their house and the thirst for conquest. As the leader of one of these factions, you must make landfall, then set up spice mines while building weapons and launching raids on your opposition. Your ultimate goal is to refine enough spice into the cosmic energy known as Girl Power to open a portal to your faction's homeworld and summon the avatar of your god-queen.

The five houses of *Spiceworld: Legacy*:

House Baby: Dressed in powder-blue plasteel, the fast-breeding acolytes of House Baby win their battles through strength of numbers, believing quantity has a quality all of its own.

House Ginger: In their red battle harness, borne aloft by their gleaming crimson rocket boots, the howling death squads of House Ginger are swift, ruthless and unmatched in single combat.

House Posh: Clad in black leather and glistening cloaking fields, the mirthless assassins of House Posh are masters of stealth, felling enemies with poisoned stilettos before an alarm can be raised.

House Scary: With their trained war-cats and flowing leopard cloaks, the battle sisters of House Scary are experts in psychological warfare, overwhelming their opponents with fear before battle.

House Sporty: Clanking in massive white-striped combat mechs, the stalwart warriors of House Sporty are resilient, fearless, and trained to fight on through catastrophic injuries.

VERDICT

Although somewhat basic due to the need to run on early smartphones, *Spiceworld* managed to achieve an astonishing level of tactical depth in its asymmetric multiplayer action.

"REFINE ENOUGH SPICE INTO THE COSMIC ENERGY KNOWN AS GIRL POWER TO OPEN A PORTAL TO YOUR FACTION'S HOMEWORLD AND SUMMON THE AVATAR OF YOUR GOD-QUEEN."

EGG GRABBER

PARTY GAME; CONTROL ENDGAME SHITFACED BUSINESSMEN AS THEY STRUGGLE ON ALL FOURS TO EAT SCOTCH EGGS OFF THE FLOOR OF A BUDGET HOTEL.

YEAR
2008

GENRE
Desperation / Party Game

DEVELOPER
Pixelgits

FORMAT
Nintendo Wii

They say there's nothing new under the sun. But under the dim lights of a cheap hotel, as you search a cigarette-burned carpet for scotch eggs on your hands and knees, it's a different story. While Pixelgits' *Egg Grabber* bore echoes of other games mentioned in this collection (the ravening, grotesque businessmen of *Buffet Lords*, the weird ovoid obsession of *Bread Egg Redemption*, and the staggering inebriation of *Pissed Bushido*, among others), what it lost in originality of theme it more than made up for in sheer, uncomplicated fun. It was, it's fair to say, a game best played with people who were completely out of their minds: in the right atmosphere, which generally meant 2am at a particularly weapons-grade party, it was about as satisfying as a game could be. Play was very simple – players would first generate their own businessman, using a system of sliders and grab-and-stretch controls to create the most lumpen monstrosities imaginable, then play a warm-up game in which their brutish entrepreneurs hoovered up wine together while telling lies about deals. Then it was straight into the action – the scene would transition to a shitty hotel room, where the businessmen would lumber around attempting to grab and consume the scotch eggs being hurled in on plates via a hatch in the wall. The controls were erratic, the characters' movements were massively loaded with inertia and excess momentum, and balance was a nightmare to maintain. Plus, when a player lost their footing (and it was always a question of *when*, not *if*), that was that – it was hands and knees from then on. At this stage of play, the game's hit detection got deliberately sloppy, too; a mistimed button press could mean players trying to eat shards of smashed plate instead of eggs or – if they initiated the eating action too near another businessman – gnawing ineffectually on the other person's hands, shoes or long, rubbery nose. This lead to hilariously clumsy fights, with scotch eggs being ground into foreheads and ties becoming tangled in braces, until everyone's sobriety meter completely bottomed out and caused them to slump forward in blackout. And that was it – the scores were tallied and a trophy appeared with someone's face on, accompanied by a sad fanfare. Could you honestly ask more of a game?

VERDICT

Short, sweet and to the point, *Egg Grabber* was a paragon of egg-themed party games.

"LUMBER AROUND ATTEMPTING TO GRAB AND CONSUME THE SCOTCH EGGS BEING HURLED IN ON PLATES VIA A HATCH IN THE WALL."

68 WOLFGLANCE TYCOON

MANAGEMENT RPG: YOU HAVE A WOLF IN THE BACK ROOM OF A DINGY PUB. CHARGE PUNTERS 50P TO HAVE A LOOK AT IT SO YOU CAN AFFORD MORE ANIMALS.

YEAR
2008

GENRE
The Tragedy of Mankind's Separation From Nature / Management

DEVELOPER
Snake Emperor Games

FORMAT
PC Core 2 Duo 2.7

"*Oi mate, fancy a quick look at a wolf?*" At the start of 2008, few suspected this phrase would become not just emblematic of the burgeoning indie game scene, but a globally recognised meme in its own right. Nevertheless, with those nine words, a phenomenon was born. At first glance, *Wolfglance Tycoon* was rather basic: you were a glum man who had somehow obtained a wolf, and were keeping it in the back room of a pub. Sitting with a pint of tepid shandy, you would beckon other punters over, offer them a glimpse of the wolf and – should they be willing to pay 50p – lead them to have a look at it. After a day or so of this, the money would start to stack up, and you could use it to buy upgrades for the wolf viewing experience: themed costumes for the wolf, exciting murals and props for its room, or better meat to keep it from getting cross. This in turn would bring more people to the pub, and justify a higher asking price for viewings – soon enough, you'd have enough cash on your hands to think about hiring staff, buying more animals, or bribing the local council to turn a blind eye to what was rapidly amounting to an unlicensed zoo. By the late game, a player might be running a series of viewing experiences in up to twelve backrooms, store cupboards and sheds: you could get a pygmy hippo or a boa constrictor for the gent's loos, and keep a camel in the garden if you had the staff to keep an eye on it. The game always ended in collapse of one kind of another, and that's a good thing, as it's really just not okay to keep wild animals in a pub. But it didn't really matter – unlike in most management games, the joy of *Wolfglance* was never really about the methodical building of order and complexity from nothing. In fact, you could argue that the game's real message was a subversion of this civilising impulse. The real magic was in its mood; in its subdued, painterly visuals and its strangely poignant procedurally generated dialogue; it managed to speak volumes about human wonder, and the disconnect between civilised and wild environments. While it never hammered the point home, this was a deeply thoughtful and exploratory game that left you thinking for weeks after completion.

VERDICT

After an hour or so playing *Wolfglance Tycoon*, you'll wonder if we aren't all in a dismal pub, longing for a peek at the wild – no matter the cost.

"SUBDUED, PAINTERLY VISUALS AND STRANGELY POIGNANT PROCEDURALLY GENERATED DIALOGUE."

69 GRUDZAK, ROASTMASTER

TOUCHSCREEN GAME WHERE YOU PLAY A MIGHTY ORC CHIEFTAIN, ENSLAVED AND FORCED TO MAN THE COUNTER AT A MIDLANDS CARVERY RESTAURANT.

YEAR
2009

GENRE
Fantasy and Sunday Roasts / Fighting

DEVELOPER
Harmless Japes

FORMAT
Mobile, Tablet

Poor old Grudzak. As the splendid opening animation of his game tells us, he was so happy in his job as warmaster for the Deathboars, the ruling orc clan on the barbaric world of Korzaath. He had a mighty husband, three mighty daughters, and a mighty hyena which brought him his mighty pipe and his mighty slippers each night. But his rival, the fiendish warlock Groothnar, could not abide his success. Making a deal with the demon To'beh, a glowering giant with a three-cornered hat, Groothnar had Grudzak banished to a life of servitude in a nightmare world. That nightmare world was our own, and Grudzak's place of imprisonment was a carvery restaurant on the Walsall Broadway, deep in the windswept reaches of the UK's West Midlands. This is where we join him, shackled to a serving counter with osmium manacles, as he prepares to cater to the Sunday rush. Using touchscreen controls to guide Grudzak's slicing and hacking, we must carve the appropriate cuts from a row of roast meats, meeting an unending stream of demands from sunken-eyed, hard-faced pensioners. The patrons are ravenous, and their orders come thick and fast – should Grudzak make even a single mistake, he faces the lash from To'beh, who looms like a wall of shadow behind him. Yet if Grudzak completes the orders faster than commanded, he earns crystals from a mischievous gravy sprite – and when he collects enough crystals, he may request a trial by combat from his captor. These trials switch the game to a side-on, turn-based fighter, where Grudzak can use moves learned at the carvery counter to hew his foes. These foes grow harder as the game advances. First, Grudzak must fell the three terrible Spirits of the Roast: a dire turkey with razor talons, an iron-bristled boar the size of a rhino, and a blood-red ox that drips with scalding juices. Once these are defeated, he may take on To'beh himself – first in the guise of a mortal giant wielding a fork and blade, second as a meat golem commanding a swarm of pensioners in thrall, and thirdly as a cosmic behemoth with a crown of stars. Once To'beh is defeated, Grudzak is free to return to Korzaath and face down Groothnar.

VERDICT

Barbaric as he is, there's something intensely likeable about Grudzak, and players can't help but feel compelled to get him back home, no matter how much dry turkey breast it takes.

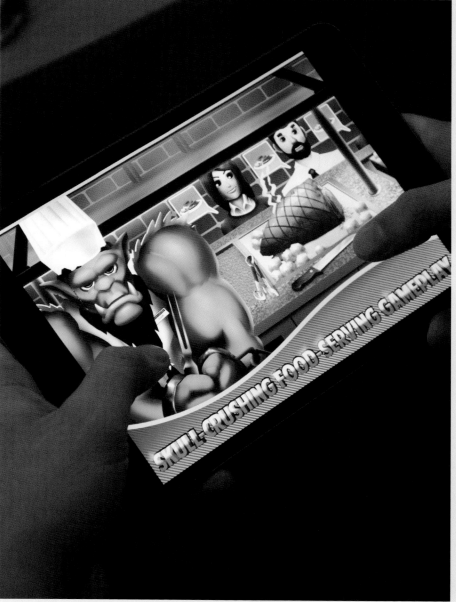

"CARVE THE APPROPRIATE CUTS FROM A ROW OF ROAST MEATS, MEETING AN UNENDING STREAM OF DEMANDS FROM SUNKEN-EYED, HARD-FACED PENSIONERS."

70

SCOUSE DRACULA

AWARD-WINNING INTERACTIVE FICTION ADAPTATION OF THE TIMELESS NARRATIVE ARCHETYPE.

YEAR
2009

GENRE
Scouse Dracula / Adventure

DEVELOPER
Storytell Games

FORMAT
PC Core 2 Duo 2.8

It's said there are only so many stories in the world – man versus nature, man versus God, man versus himself, and so on. Perhaps no archetype is so pervasive, however, as that of Scouse Dracula. This century alone, Hollywood has tackled the formula three times, and with *The Mersey Ran Red* about to hit the West End after a wild run on Broadway, it's not going away anytime soon. It seems the idea of 'Dracula, but he's from Liverpool' is a concept so fundamentally ingrained in the human psyche that we can't help but retell his story again and again. In 2009 Storytell Games, famed for reinvigorating the adventure genre through use of classic properties such as *Roadhouse* and *Showgirls*, took their turn to have a crack at the Scouse whip. Of course, the games industry had tried to tackle the subject before, with mixed results – 1986's *Scouse Dracula's Castle* for the NES was little more than a run-of-the-mill platformer, while the 1995 mystery game *A Mist Over Anfield*, despite tackling the subject matter in depth, came across as flaccid and lacking in heart. Storytell, however, managed to utterly smash the concept into the back of the digital net with their narrative masterpiece. Set in the early 1990s, it reimagined the count along the lines of Derek Hatton in his prime; a man with political leanings as red as his undying thirst for blood. Instead of being a ghoulish, aristocratic predator, Storytell's hero was a man of the people who – much like his fellow Scousers – could not abide the sight of the sun. By day, he lurked in his council flat, occasionally peering out from its heavy curtains to look broodingly on the world beyond. By night, however, he roamed the Merseyside region in his ghost-powered taxi, picking up fares and seeking out redtop tabloid readers to slake his thirst. But beneath this nocturnal crusade was a deeper tragedy: Drac was ever on the lookout for his girlfriend Sarah, who he had lost contact with after a passionate dockside liaison in the closing years of the nineteenth century. One night, after slaying a journalist in a rainy alley, he finds a photograph in the pocket of their mac that looks identical to his lost love, and his real hunt begins.

VERDICT

Enthralling, romantic and deeply political, *Scouse Dracula* showed that games can go toe-to-toe with any other medium when it comes to telling classic stories.

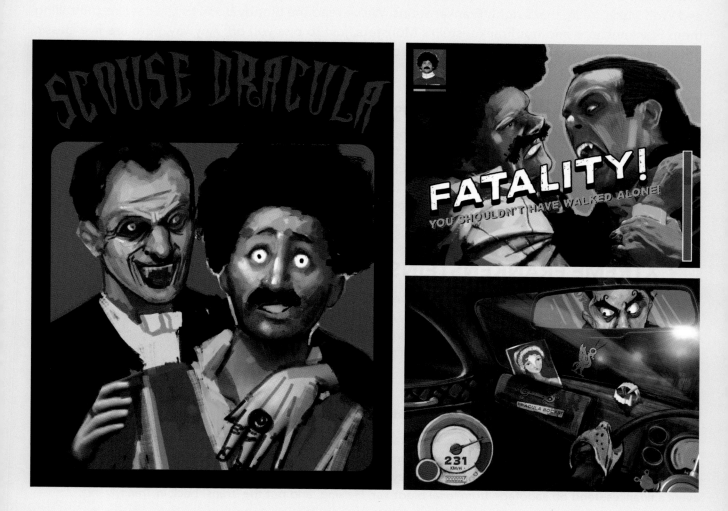

"DRACULA, BUT HE'S FROM LIVERPOOL."

DRACULAS, FRANKENSTEINS AND WOLF MANS

While it's hard to beat *Scouse Dracula* when it comes to hard-hitting vampire narratives, it's important not to forget the broad and rich thematic territory of Draculas in general. And of course, Draculas themselves are just part of a wider world of knackered horror tropes including Frankensteins, Mummies and Wolf Mans. Yeah, that's right: Frankensteins. We've read the bloody book too, but we're still calling them Frankensteins and not Frankenstein's Monsters, *just to piss you off*. Anyway, here are five classic titles that have tackled the lightning-ravaged, creaking-doored realm of generic horror over the years:

01 DRACULA 2083 // Dukes of Spook, 2002

This retro cyberpunk platformer, dripping with colourful pixel art, starred a version of Dracula with mirror shades, a backwards baseball cap, and a cybernetic arm that fired metal bats. Over the course of the Count's romp through a futuristic LA, he could call on the aid of DJ Mummy (an embalmed pharaoh who summoned dancing zombies to fight foes), Hoverboard Frankenstein (a bodacious cyborg corpse on a rocket surfboard) and the Glitchwolf (a bipedal wolf who could turn into a cloud of corrupted visuals to delete enemies from the game).

02 XTREME FRANKENSTEINS // Gnarlsoft, 2004

In this laid-back extreme sports game, players were in control of a groaning boltneck on a skateboard, and challenged to execute as many sweet tricks as they could in a storm-blasted gothic skatepark. Special skills could be gained from sewing on body parts from famous pro-skaters, while catching sufficient air would result in being struck by lightning, providing the power to pull off totally sick combo moves.

03 OUT FOR THE COUNT // Iridis Entertainment, 2015

It's springtime in the Carpathian mountains, and Dracula has commissioned you to run his domain's very first Pride parade. And while this is a land of spooky monsters, it's time to show the world that even spooky monsters can be whoever they want to be, and love whoever they want to love. As such, it'll come down to you to manage the event's finances, fend off sabotage from local bigot Van Helsing, and put the 'trans' back in Transylvania.

04 STAKES ON A PLANE // Rustled Jimmy Productions, 2007

You play a vampire hunter aboard a jumbo jet in this tense mystery game, trying to identify and slay twelve vampires who have stowed away on a transatlantic flight before they can feed on too many passengers. While the withered Nosferatu lurking in the plane's hold is fairly easy to seek out and put an end to, some of the vampires are hiding in plain sight amongst the human passengers – and if you put a stake through the heart of an innocent customer by mistake, it's game over.

05 VERDUN WEREWOLF // Thudrock Games, 2017

In this WWI horror FPS, you play the role of an officer on the Western Front who comes from a noble family long-cursed with lycanthropy. Desperate to protect your men while keeping your foul secret hidden, you must make careful choices about when to transform, and how to cope when the urge to feed becomes too strong. A charge on enemy lines, for example, provides the perfect cover, and the famous sequence inside a German machine gun nest has already become notorious as one of the most shocking moments in gaming history.

2010
ONWARDS

71

RISK EVERYTHING

FPS FROM THE PERSPECTIVE OF A SOLDIER IN A GAME OF RISK. LIVE THE MADNESS AS TEN MILLION MEN INVADE AUSTRALIA FOR NO REASON.

YEAR
2010

GENRE
The Horror of War / FPS

DEVELOPER
Fistfight Studios

FORMAT
PC Core i3, Xbox 360

I think anyone would agree that war is a pretty terrible thing. But it could be worse. It could be *Risk*. Those who've played the board game know the drill: players are given random territories around the world, and use them as springboards to capture arbitrary objectives. They do this with ever-escalating numbers of troops, and will squander them to the last man in fruitless attempts to conquer territories they 'need.' *Risk Everything*'s campaign begins in the blasted tundra of Irkutsk, Eastern Siberia. As a Blue Army soldier, you march as part of a million-man blitzkrieg across all of Eurasia; once Spain is secured, orders are received that Eastern Australia must be captured, and a 10,000 mile odyssey begins immediately. After countless pitched battles, you arrive in Papua New Guinea, only for you and ten million other men to attempt a crossing of the Torres Strait – under torrential artillery fire. When the fight is done, the survivors are counted – only 3,000 remain standing to witness a mammoth Red Army dropship settle in the grey distance over the sea. Twenty million enemy troops are disgorged, and yet again, the carnage begins. Of course, the horror is diminished slightly by everyone being made of plastic – but not by much: the screams of the dying are human enough. Plus, every time you die (on average, every six seconds) you spawn as another soldier, making the game a rapid-fire montage of final moments. Sometimes, you and four comrades will be merged into a giant horse; sometimes, a whole platoon will be lumped together into a gun. And there is never any explanation for what is happening – yours, indeed, is not to reason why. Your commanders will sometimes give speeches, but they are essentially apologies for the whims of the gods. Indeed, it is the gods who bring about the game's end. As the red troopers storm up the beach, a conflagration erupts in heaven; the daughter of the Celestial Family, your patron, has accused her father of cheating. He insists he is merely following a house rule, but events spiral out of control – fistfuls of mountainous dice plummet from the sky, smashing battalions asunder, and countless millions of troops are crash-landed in for a ghastly final battle.

VERDICT

Ostensibly a dark comedy about what would happen if we experienced board games from the point of view of the pieces, *Risk Everything* gets less funny when you think about WWI.

"THE HORROR IS DIMINISHED SLIGHTLY BY EVERYONE BEING MADE OF PLASTIC – BUT NOT BY MUCH."

72 BMX CRUSADERS

HISTORICAL EXTREME SPORTS MMO FOR MOBILE; 1,000 MOUNTAIN BIKES HAVE APPEARED IN POPE URBAN II'S VATICAN, AND HAVE ENABLED A WHOLE NEW MODE OF WARFARE.

YEAR
2010

GENRE
Cycling Knights / Action

DEVELOPER
Zipline Wildebeest Games

FORMAT
Smartphone

Sometimes, when a game goes into development hell, it can come out the other side as a very different animal indeed. The genesis of *BMX Crusaders* was a historical 'what if?' question – what if 1,000 modern mountain bikes had appeared inexplicably in medieval Europe? The team at Zipline Wildebeest planned to answer this question via an epic RPG, written by Hollywood screenwriters in conjunction with historians, pro-cyclists and experts in medieval martial arts. Early concept art was incredible, showing gilded bikes encrusted with religious iconography hung on the walls of cathedrals, and knights taking to the battlefields of the Hundred Years War astride smith-forged replicas of modern bicycles. But then the financial crisis of 2008 hit, and Zipline had to make huge layoffs – *Crusaders* was mothballed, and all staff who survived the purge were moved to work on the company's cash cow series about people being sick, *Chunder Champs*. Nevertheless, in early 2010, the decision was made to revive *Crusaders*. *Quadbike Sorcerer II* had just hit shelves and was making a fortune, so Zipline's shareholders were anxious to get something released quick, before the trend for extreme sports in an archaic setting ran its course. A grim-faced meeting was held to decide what the quickest way of turning the embryonic *BMX Crusaders* into a minimum viable commercial product was, and the answer was unanimous: smash it out as a mobile game riddled with microtransactions, and hope for the best. This mortified project leader Fiona Blop, who had championed the original project, but there was no time to argue, so she set to work. Just six months later, *BMX Crusaders* was released – and it was horrendous. Code had been ripped wholesale from a 1985 arcade game about paper delivery, and so gameplay involved trundling a knight through an endless maze of desert encampments and… delivering newspapers. It made no sense at all. But crucially, it made a fucking fortune.

VERDICT

Despite being a flimsy shadow of the powerhouse it was originally slated to be, *BMX Crusaders* was a resounding success, birthing spin-offs such as *Skateboard Saladin* and *Richard the Basejumping Lionheart*. It remains a solid example of how 'good' can mean very different things for artists and salespeople.

"AN ENDLESS MAZE OF DESERT ENCAMPMENTS AND...
DELIVERING NEWSPAPERS."

73 HUNGRY HUNGRY HIPPOS CRISIS

SQUAD-BASED SHOOTER – DEFEND LONDON AGAINST FOUR INSATIABLE HIPPOS THAT GET BIGGER AND BIGGER THE MORE THEY EAT.

YEAR
2010

GENRE
Hippocalypse / FPS

DEVELOPER
Riot Keg Entertainment

FORMAT
PC Core i3, Playstation 3, Xbox 360

The last decade has seen Hollywood increasingly eschew original ideas in favour of endless risk-averse remakes and reboots, so it was little surprise when games took the same route. Indeed, 2010's biggest game was *Hungry Hungry Hippos Crisis*, which turned a children's game from 1978 into a high-octane kaiju thriller. The premise was glorious: terrorists have unleashed four hippos into the heart of London, infected with a nanoplague that drives them mad with hunger, brings their skin out in unnatural colours, and makes them larger and larger the more they eat. You are hippo biologist Safi Farooqi, helicoptered in with an SAS squad as the Army loses control of the situation, in a last ditch attempt to contain the hippos. After a series of initial missions where your squad must evacuate civilians and collect information on the hippos against a backdrop of gigascale carnage, the game focuses on the preparation and execution of four increasingly immense boss battles, each of which takes more than an hour of playtime to complete.

The four boss battles from *Hungry Hungry Hippos Crisis*:

Henry Hippo (blue): Henry, the weakling of the brood, is loose on Oxford Street – after initially firing appetite suppressants into the maw of the beast, you must coordinate with Army units to net the titan and sedate it, before transporting it to the Thames as bait for one its fellows.

Harry Hippo (yellow): With Henry restrained at London Bridge, cannibal behemoth Harry is lured into the Thames. After a helicopter gunship segment, and a tense underwater struggle to wound the beast, the killing blow is struck with the guns of decommissioned battleship *HMS Belfast*.

Homer Hippo (green): While the fight has been raging, phlegmatic Homer has moved to the city's outskirts,where he has eaten himself vast – you must ride around an Ealing industrial estate in a jeep, distracting him long enough for a fighter strike to be called in.

Happy Hippo (purple): The colossal Happy is moving towards the Dungeness B nuclear power plant in Kent – if she manages to eat the main reactor, she will grow beyond human control. You must pursue the beast with a column of tanks, steering it away from population centres, then confront it and leap into its jaws with a tactical nuclear weapon in a final sacrifice.

VERDICT

Fun, fun, fun by the ton, ton, ton.

"HUNGRY HUNGRY HIPPOS CRISIS TURNED A CHILDREN'S GAME FROM 1978 INTO A HIGH-OCTANE KAIJU THRILLER."

THE CRISTAL MAZE

PHONE GAME ABOUT AN ARISTOCRATIC LUSH, TRYING TO NEGOTIATE A MONSTER-CRAMMED LABYRINTH WHILE ABSOLUTELY LEATHERED ON CHAMPAGNE.

YEAR
2011

GENRE
Privilege / Dungeon Crawl

DEVELOPER
Fifth Estate Games

FORMAT
Smartphone, Tablet

The advent of punishingly hard games without save states has built the phrase 'losing is fun' into something of a mantra for masochist gamers, but never has it been more apt than in the case of *The Cristal Maze*. In this mobile game, where players tilt their phone to accentuate the bladdered stumbling of a toff in order to negotiate a winding dungeon, there's nothing more satisfying than watching the protagonist stagger into an agonising death. Seriously, the guy is impossible to like. He's so gurningly posh he can't tie his own shoelaces, and every time he quacks a glop of sick, he barks angrily for someone to clean it up. When this attracts the attention of a glowering ogre with a club, it's hard not to mutter "good riddance." Likewise, when a mistimed sprint causes him to shit down his leg, shriek "oh bother!" and wade into a spider's web, you can't help but grin. The man is so thoroughly convinced he was born to rule that the labyrinth holds no fear for him – if anything, he's irritated that its denizens aren't treating him with more deference. And as his shepherd through the catacombs, one soon adopts the smouldering resentment of a put-upon butler: loyal to their employer out of a sense of professionalism, but without a shred of compassion for their fate. Indeed, when Master Cuthbert reaches the dungeon's final level, it's with some schadenfreude that we watch him waggle his fingers in avarice over the treasure chest at its heart, only to find it contains but a single scrap of yellowed paper. As he reads the note, which coldly informs him that his estate and all of his assets have been requisitioned by goblins, the sudden collapse of his face into sobriety is more beautiful than any sunset. The game's final sequence, in which Cuthbert runs shrieking back into the maze, waving his cane in fury, can be replayed as many times as the player desires.

VERDICT

As a piece of casual gaming, *The Cristal Maze* is a win-win. Played straight, its gyroscope mechanics give even the most dextrous hands a run for their money, as negotiating the labyrinth takes real skill. Nevertheless, it's equally fun to play like an absolute bastard, just for the cathartic thrill of seeing a very unpleasant rich man get flattened by beasts in a nightmare world.

BILE LEVEL
URINE LEVEL
HICCUP VOLUME

you are:
BLADDERED

SCORE:
108,050

BALANCE METER
hiccup volume too high:
find the vol-au-vents

"THERE'S NOTHING MORE SATISFYING THAN WATCHING THE PROTAGONIST STAGGER INTO AN AGONISING DEATH."

75 90s GOTH SOCCER

LIKE ANY HIGH END FOOTBALL SIM BUT WITH LOADS MORE VINYL AND FAKE VAMPIRE TEETH, PLUS A POUNDING INDUSTRIAL SOUNDTRACK.

YEAR
2011

GENRE
Dark Pain / Football

DEVELOPER
Black Orb Developments

FORMAT
PlayStation 3

At its heart, *90s Goth Soccer* was an incredibly competent, straight-laced football game. Mechanically, in fact, it was identical to the sort of game that two lads might fire up after returning from the pub, cracking open a couple of tins of Fosters, and volleying around some light-hearted banter about each other's mums. But it was programmed by a company full of ultragoths, and it's fair to say it showed. The footballers were all dressed in lace-collared shirts, New Rocks and velvet capes, while the fans in the stands were straight out of Camden High Street in 1998. Each match was accompanied by deafening belters from NIN, KMFDM and other bands with acronyms for names, and commentary was provided by a raven-haired beauty with a lip ring, in the form of whispered, near-meaningless poetry. It may not have been a big commercial success, but it's hard to feel anything but love for a game where sliding tackles result in explosions of ravens.

Around, all around, the midfielders gather
My sickness grows as Scholes makes the pass
A miasma of blackness; dark perceptions of Teddy Sheringham
An unstoppable force, in possession of the ball
Yet again. It crushes me, and darkly his
Essence drips
To the dead grass.
In a haze of forwards, I condemn you
In numbness he tries to run
While the goal hovers close
Now alone, his supplication falls upon screaming fans
This is football.

– Example commentary from *90s Goth Soccer*

VERDICT

90s Goth Soccer was objectively the best football game of its generation, resulting in the glorious spectacle of millions of lads having to grudgingly come to terms with its aesthetic.

"A GAME WHERE SLIDING TACKLES RESULT IN EXPLOSIONS OF RAVENS."

FOOTBALL GAMES

Perhaps no game in the history of sports simulation has subverted the expectations of its playerbase as profoundly as *90s Goth Soccer*. Nevertheless, there have been countless other football games that chose to forego tradition in favour of more… esoteric interpretations of the beautiful game. Here are some that really stood out from the pack:

01 GAOL! // Shy Thomas Games, 1998

Ultra-slick football game set in a medieval prison, where the ball is a pig's heart full of sawdust and the players are lepers in gaily coloured rags. The commentary is in early Middle English, random players get executed at halftime, and French armies occasionally invade the pitch. Gadzooks!

02 NARCOLEPSY FOOTBALL 3 // Bumblebeast, 2002

Dutch football legend Johan Cruyff said that "you play football with your head, and your legs are there to help you." That's why this sleepy sports sim is a fucking nightmare, as any one of your players may fall asleep at any moment. Rapid passing is essential once you notice a midfielder getting the nods, and penalty shoot-outs are even more tense than usual.

03 STARGOALS 8 MILLION // Glass Sandwich Productions, 2010

Play a striker for a plucky astro-football team in this physics-heavy, upbeat sci-fi sports sim. Training levels take place on Earth against a team of cheery Irish robots, but things get more complicated when matches take place under Jovian gravity, on a ball of frozen methane in the far reaches of the Kuiper belt, or on the reality-borgling fringes of a black hole. Equally, fixtures against cephalopod warriors with fifteen feet, or avian warriors who can control the ball with their minds, don't help with the game's Everestian difficulty curve.

04 HARRY SCREAMPAL // Codebrawlers, 2017

This charming educational VR app for aspiring football fans sat players in an imaginary football stadium, alongside an affable hulk called Harry with an encyclopedic knowledge of team-based shouting. This brutish sensei would select classic matches for the two of you to view, then coach you on what to bellow, and when, in order to seem like a proper fan. Immensely affirming.

05 THE HAIRDRYER TREATMENT // Rollicking Misadventures, 2016

A football management sim with a difference, this intense game came complete with a model of a human head, wired with volume, pressure and motion sensors. With action taking place entirely at halftime, *The Hairdryer Treatment* was all about choosing the right players to bollock, then getting right up in their faces and screaming at them to be better at football.

06 PROFOUND EVOLUTION SOCCER // Boar Symbol Studios, 2003

One fair criticism of football is that there isn't a huge amount of genetic or cybernetic modification to players, with the possible exception of French midfielder N'golo Kante. All that changed in *PES*, where you could give your players terrible augmentations such as jet engine chests, heads that fire at other players or giant flapping feet, just for the sake of seeing what would happen.

07 LAIRDS AY FITBA // Shabby Duncans, 1999

In this bleak RPG, set in Scotland forty years after an unspecified global catastrophe, you play the daughter of a chieftain who rules over a clan based entirely on the worship of pre-crisis football culture. Criminals are executed by having a ball kicked through their chest, while the clan goes to war in a rusted fan's coach pulled by blinded slaves. Can you convince your father to mend his ways and finally kick the violence out of football, or will you become the most dreaded of his strikers?

08 FOOTBALL 40,000 // Lost Proprietary, 2006

Dense MMO set in a baroque far future where modern Premier League sides have somehow grown into vast interstellar empires, ruled over by undying Chairman and led into battle by Managers in house-sized power armour. The game's first expansion concerned House Chelsea's attempt to build a spaceship large enough to kick a star through the 'goal' of a supermassive black hole.

09 ULTIMATE GOAL CELEBRATOR // Weeeeeeyyyy! Games, 2011

A sandbox game that's less about football, and more about setting up the most outrageous goal celebrations imaginable. With a vast array of tools and assets at your disposal, anything can happen: the striker turning suddenly and bloodily into a dragon, a pitch invasion by thousands of dancing girls, a man defeating a tiger with a trident. Whatever you like.

76

CHUKA UMUNNA'S BUNGEE SLEDGEHAMMER PANIC

DECEPTIVELY FUN, IF WEIRDLY THEMED, 8-BIT MULTIPLAYER ACTION FEATURING THE FORMER SHADOW BUSINESS SECRETARY.

YEAR
2011

GENRE
Economic Policy /
Multiplayer Combat

DEVELOPER
Unknown

FORMAT
Xbox 360, PC i3

Although this game was supposedly released to commemorate Chuka Umunna becoming the UK's shadow business secretary in 2011, it really isn't clear whether the anonymous coder behind this retro effort was a detractor or a fan of the well-known MP. On the one hand, Umunna's unsanctioned portrayal in the game is fairly positive – he plays the smiling, pixelated host of the game's motorway flyover bloodsport with some aplomb. But on the other hand: *motorway flyover bloodsport*. The mechanics are simple: each player starts atop the flyover with a ten pound sledgehammer in their hands, and a short length of bungee rope around their ankle. After a brief round of encouraging chat about the growth potential of small-to-medium enterprises in the UK, Umunna shoves them off, and the madness begins. Subtly brilliant physics modelling means that a missed swing or glancing hit can result in uncontrollable spinning, while a downward whack with a bit of bungee momentum behind it can be devastating. A winner is only eventually reeled up once all other players have stopped moving, and the round finishes with a short speech to camera from Chuka on one of a number of topics including the privatisation of postal services, the role of regulation in a competitive economy, and the importance of regional autonomy in democracy.

Kidneys spiralling out of a man's back to slap against the windscreen of a passing eighteen-wheeler? Probably not something a politician would want to be associated with, right? You would think not. Nevertheless, Labour party archive photography from 2010 has recently come to light showing Chuka in the background of a shot, clearly enjoying a pre-release demo of *CUBSP* with the Secretary of State for Business, Innovation and Skills, Vince Cable. Was Chuka somehow involved with the developers of the game? Did he make it himself? And why was he playing with an opposition MP? We may never know – while a Freedom of Information request submitted by Insurrection Publishing has confirmed that Umunna has indeed played *Sledgehammer Panic*, his office has so far declined to respond to all requests for comment. We have our suspicions.

VERDICT

Sledgehammer Panic was riotous good fun to play, if occasionally physically sickening – and it certainly got across Umunna's views on a wide range of contemporary issues.

CHUKA UMUNNA S BUNGEE
SLEDGEHAMMER PANIC

"SUBTLY BRILLIANT PHYSICS MODELLING MEANS THAT A MISSED SWING OR GLANCING HIT CAN RESULT IN UNCONTROLLABLE SPINNING."

77

TONY HAWK'S FUTURISTIC HYPERWAR SKATER 8

SKATE ALONG THE DECKS OF MASSIVE DUELLING STARSHIPS, AVOIDING ARTILLERY FIRE AND BOARDING ACTIONS, IN THIS EXHILARATING SPORTS TITLE.

YEAR
2012

GENRE
Space Combat / Extreme Sports

DEVELOPER
Owl World Entertainment

FORMAT
Xbox 360, PlayStation 3, PC

Since the release of the original in 1999, the *Tony Hawk's Futuristic Hyperwar Skater* series has continued to go from strength to strength. Its eighth installment, published in 2012, broke from the chain of sequels to offer an HD remake of *THFHS1*, amping up the hyperkinetic bombast of its starship duels to the processing limits of modern hardware. Of course, its release saw the usual chorus of dusty old voices moan the question "why not just set it in a skate park?" but the answer was ever the same: because without the futuristic hyperwar, it wouldn't be *Tony Hawk's Futuristic* fucking *Hyperwar Skater*, would it? The series' charm has always been about the transcendental disconnect between laid back US skate culture and baroque military science fiction, and long may that remain the case. After all, there's nothing quite like grinding along the loading rails of a plasma torpedo tube, before ollie-ing onto the nose of the projectile and riding it across the howling void towards a city-sized battleship and kick-flipping your way out of the resultant impact. With the huge variety of floating debris, strange gravity effects and architectural complexity in play, it's just hard to beat a gigaton capital ship engagement when it comes to an interesting arena for skating in. The beauty of it all is only increased by how little the player character has to do with the madness going on around them. Tony and the various other skate legends portrayed in the game (as well as the roster of astronauts added for the remake), glide serenely through the apoplexy of interstellar combat without a care for its participants or their struggle; all they want is to grab some sweet, sweet air (or vacuum) and listen to the half-arsed punk anthems blaring out over the sound of railgun fire. In one memorable level from *THFHS8*, a beetle-like Kor'Tavorr Gas Baron has donned his ten-thousand-year-old war armour and is leading a mass boarding action across the hull of a stricken enemy brood-carrier in order to claim a rival throne. All that matters to Tony, however, is what kind of gnarly trick he can pull off on the Baron's extravagant helm. If we all took this approach to conflict and strife, maybe the world would be a better place.

VERDICT

THFHS8 was a return to glory for this proud workhorse of a series, showcasing the core qualities that made the original a hit, while blending in the visual intoxication of next-gen graphics.

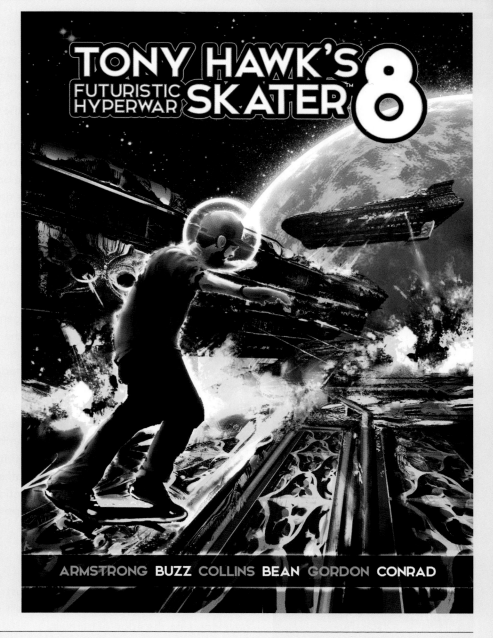

"THE BEAUTY OF IT ALL IS ONLY INCREASED BY HOW LITTLE THE PLAYER CHARACTER HAS TO DO WITH THE MADNESS GOING ON AROUND THEM."

78

THE WOLF SCHOOL PROPHECIES

FINALLY, A DECENT GAME LICENSED ON THE WOLF SCHOOL FRANCHISE. HEART-CRUNCHING, RAPTUROUS FPS ACTION WITH PLENTY OF NODS FOR SUPERFANS.

YEAR
2012

GENRE
Wolves / School

DEVELOPER
The Venison Parallax

FORMAT
Xbox 360, PC

The longer the world went without a proper *Wolf School* game, the more of a headache the prospect of making one became. By 2012, the *Wolf School* fandom – or 'Wolfies,' to use their parlance – had split into several bitterly divided camps. Some were fans of the original UK series, with its low budget reliance on stock footage of wolves, while others stood by the US remake, which reinterpreted the premise as a CG-heavy tale of high school lycanthropy. Others shunned the TV treatments of the lupoverse entirely, championing instead the 1996 movie and its sequels, which featured human actors overlaid with the rotoscoped heads of trained wolves. To favour any one of these options would be to alienate the fans of the others, and so when the announcement came from The Venison Parallax in 2001 that a game was in the works, few envied them. Sure, they went on to drop the hit of the year with *Thomas the War Engine* in 2005 (p. 144), but was tackling *Wolf School* an act of towering hubris too far? The next eleven years seemed to suggest it very much had been, as the benighted project went through three changes of engine, countless leadership changes, and at least two complete returns to the drawing board. As the project's ten-year anniversary came and went, VP's assurances that the game would be "done when it's done" were beginning to wear thin. But then the unthinkable happened – at 2012's E3 expo, lead developer Buster Chestguts took to the stage to announce the game's release in November, and proceeded to drop five minutes of demo footage. At first, the audience was silent except for nervous giggles, expecting an utter trainwreck to unfold. But as the game's ultra-fluid gunplay and pure revelry in *Wolf School* lore became apparent, jaws dropped. At the end of the demo, as a shaft of light illuminated the terrible form of Professor Greymane, the crowd held their breath. Padding towards the camera, the headmaster growled his infamous line, "Have you done your maths homework?" and the cheers nearly blew the roof off the Los Angeles Convention Centre. There was no question – The Venison Parallax had achieved the impossible, and united the Wolfies at last.

VERDICT

The Wolf School Prophecies wasn't just a technical achievement; it was a Herculean act of perseverance that will stand forever as an inspiration to developers on the edge of burnout.

LEVEL UP!

235 ♥ 22

"ULTRA-FLUID GUNPLAY AND PURE REVELRY IN *WOLF SCHOOL* LORE."

79 CRUMPLEZONE

WHIMSICAL SHOOTER ABOUT HIGH-TECH URBAN WARFARE, BUT THE MECHAS ARE CARDBOARD, THE GUNS FIRE PAINTBALLS, AND THE COMBATANTS ARE KIDS HAVING THE BEST SUMMER HOLIDAY OF THEIR LIVES.

YEAR
2012

GENRE
Imagination / FPS

DEVELOPER
Stack Overflow Games

FORMAT
Xbox 360, PlayStation 3

While *The Wolf School Prophecies* had offered a breath of fresh air for the industry in more ways than one, the wider gaming world was beginning to feel in desperate need of innovation by 2012. First person shooters were dominating the market on console and PC, and all seemed to occupy the same thematic territory: grunting, bulging men unloading massive guns into foreigners in the name of liberty, freedom, and increasingly desperate conceptions of masculine identity. Something needed to change, and *Crumplezone* was the first crack in the dam. Set in a sleepy Midwestern suburb, it told the story of Madi and Jake, eleven-year-old twins with a long, hot summer ahead of them, and nothing much to do. When they find a massive pile of cardboard behind a local supermarket, Madi hatches a plan – they will round up all the kids from the neighbourhood, divide up the cardboard, and have a war. The campaign that followed – which could be played from the POV of either Madi's or Jake's factions – took place in an amalgam of the twins' neighbourhood and their imaginations; houses could be houses, or they could be fortified skyscrapers, depending on the needs of the mission. Jake's super-heavy command tank, despite being carried along by six other kids, clanked and belched smoke as if it were a 100-ton war machine. Water balloons made the sound of Molotov cocktails despite only making things soggy, and paintballs slammed into cardboard with the sound of steel on steel. Gameplay was frenetic, difficult, and required the same skill and reflexes of any other shooter on the market – but here's the thing: nobody got hurt. It was a bold departure from the norm, and if the game hadn't been so bloody awesome to play, it could have backfired badly. But as it was, it sparked a wide cultural movement towards non-violent action games, such as 2013's *Laser Ghosts*, 2014's multicoloured vomit-fest *Rainbow Sicks*, and 2015's *Makura Taisen*, a Japanese one-on-one battler about an international pillow-fighting tournament.

VERDICT

For gamers with itchy trigger fingers who were nonetheless sick of lantern-jawed commandos and tiresomely hench marines, *Crumplezone* was a hobby-saving tonic.

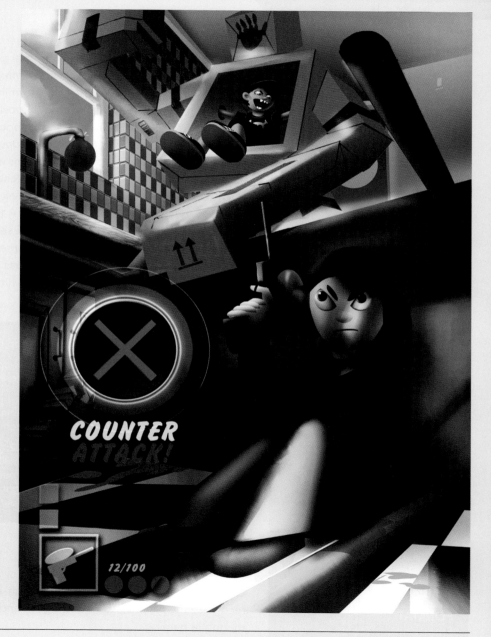

"GAMEPLAY WAS FRENETIC, DIFFICULT, AND REQUIRED THE SAME SKILL AND REFLEXES OF ANY OTHER SHOOTER ON THE MARKET."

80 KOMODO FLAGONS

ONE PUB, SIXTEEN MASSIVE LIZARDS: HAVE YOU GOT WHAT IT TAKES TO KEEP THEM ALL COMPLETELY SHITFACED?

YEAR
2013

GENRE
Lizards / Barkeeping

DEVELOPER
FunBlob Studios

FORMAT
Smartphone, Tablet

Phone games need to be quick, easy to learn, and horribly addictive to succeed. What they don't need, however, is any real genius in the plot department. That's why, when app studio FunBlob was commissioned to put together the Next Big Thing for smartphones, the brainstorming meeting didn't last long. "Pissed lizards," growled art director Sidney Bloosh, from his hangover nest beneath the table. "You get big lizards pissed on booze," he snapped, when questioned further, and that was that: *Komodo Flagons* was born. Nevertheless, for all the indelicacy of its founding premise, *Flagons* was a game of surprising complexity – as well as classic touchscreen control, it challenged players with tilt sensor and voice recognition mechanics in their quest to keep a gang of reptiles totally walloped on hooch. It wasn't flawless – the pint-balancing mini game was notoriously buggy, and an ill-advised RPG segment led to a genuinely menacing bit where a heavily lagered crocodile corners you by some fruit machines and calls you a wanker for a full hour – but it was more than worth the asking price of three quid, and soon became the smash hit FunBlob had hoped for. Get those scaly boys another round!

FunBlob's next four (highly imaginative) app releases:

Ale Whales: Five flat-capped whales show up in a quiet Yorkshire pub; you must slake their leviathanic thirst for real ale before they go completely moby and trash the place.

Grog Frogs: You are a magic fairy, running a cocktail bar for tiny frogs. Unfortunately, you still have to get them completely smashmouthed on funjuice.

Booze Cruise Gnus/Booze Cruise Gnus 2: Wildebeested: It's the peak of the Serengeti wildebeest migration, with 1.5 million animals on the move across East Africa. You're the proprietor of the only pub en route, and must prepare for a Saturday night like no other. *BCG2* brought more of the same, with the added challenge of keeping lions and crocodiles out of the bar.

VERDICT

Okay – we admit it wasn't exactly high art, but it would be wrong not to recognise the place of *Komodo Flagons* and its spiritual sequels in the evolution of mobile gaming.

ROUND 3
00:32

35%

DRINK READY

"KEEP A GANG OF REPTILES TOTALLY WALLOPED ON HOOCH."

FIVE FINGER-SMEARED TABLET GAMES

Following the mass adoption of smartphones and tablet devices in the early years of the decade, mobile gaming has become a spectacularly lucrative area for developers. With miserable commuters able to download games at the touch of a screen, the market has offered untold riches for those able to make an icon enticing enough to waste a couple of bob on. Here are five genuine treasures from this storm-tossed ocean of shit:

01 MONSTERED EXPAT 2 // Snidewinder Studios, 2014

In this nihilistic rhythm game, your job was to keep a beetroot-faced ex-stockbroker's heart going as long as possible, as he floated comatose on a lilo after a mindroasting go on the old marching powder. As the camera spiralled slowly upwards away from his charlie-blasted wreck of a body, the thud of his heart became fainter and fainter, and the beauty of the Spanish countryside took centre stage. While you could never win, it was rumoured that if you kept his ticker going until you reached the clouds, you might be lucky enough to hear one last, whispered regret.

02 ALBATROSS DENTIST // Synergy Gulch Solutions, 2013

While its icon and promotional graphics promised a goofy cartoon caper about a crazed dentist and his waiting room full of large avian patients, the reality of this game was a cruel surprise. On loading the app, the player was presented with a cartoon dental mirror and the words "Pick up the mirror to start the fun!" When they did so, the screen would cut to black, and the words "Birds don't have teeth, you fool" would swim slowly into focus. Masterful.

03 BUILDERS' TEA BURDEN // Batterblunch Software, 2015

This stressful app saw players tasked with taking a tea order from a set of scaffolding packed with roaring builders, then remembering everyone's preferences while assembling the brews in a cramped Portakabin. The memory game had a dark side as well – after dishing out the mugs, every builder whose order you had buggered up would queue up to fight you in a dusty yard full of cinderblocks and lengths of metal pipe. If you were shit at memory games *and* fighting games, *BTB* was essentially just constant punishment.

04 GANGLAND TAILOR // Gundabad Games, 2017

As a high-end tailor in London's East End during the mid-1960s, there was no avoiding the fact that organised criminals would form a significant part of your clientele. After all, who ever enjoyed a sharp suit more than a 1960s gangster? In this game, built around the twin mechanics of touch-controlled tape measure work and the selection of small talk to pass the time with clients, it was your job to take accurate fittings from towering thugs, without ever being perceived as too touchy-feely, or leading conversation into potentially dark places. The tension was constant – one press too hard in a sensitive area, or a casual remark about local police activity, could result in instant hospitalisation.

05 GURN WITH THE WIND // Honking Mayor, 2016

Essentially an interactive version of the classic grandmother warning, "If the wind changes, you'll be stuck looking like that," this extremely silly puzzler presented players with a near-perfect anatomical simulation of a human face, making a variety of ridiculous expressions. Tweaking facial muscles and nudging tissue with your thumbs, the challenge was to get the face into a state roughly resembling normalcy before the wind picked up and fixed it in position.

81

BANTELOPES

LAD-BASED SURVIVAL HORROR; WHEN A HAUNTED OUIJA BOARD TRAPS FIVE BOYS IN THE BODIES OF ANTELOPES, THEY ARE LEFT TO FEND FOR THEMSELVES ON THE PUNISHING EXPANSE OF THE SERENGETI.

YEAR
2013

GENRE
Toxic Masculinity / Nature / Horror

DEVELOPER
Smashboy North

FORMAT
Xbox One, PlayStation 4

Having played the opening level of *Bantelopes*, you'd be forgiven for throwing the disc in the woods: it's a loveless portrait of five braying twats on a safari holiday, discussing women like items in a meat raffle and constantly insulting each other to hide their all-consuming self-doubt. We follow their 'antics' from Heathrow airport to the rolling expanse of East Africa, grinding our teeth as they slap each other for BookFace videos and make carelessly racist comments about their guides. But patience was rewarded, as *Bantelopes* was merely building the lads up in order to tear them down. As the first night of the trip begins, the boys find an eerie old ouija board in their lodge, and egg each other on to have a go. Without any of them touching the board, it spells out 'WEEEYYYY, BANTER!' and a burst of light strikes them unconscious. When they awake the next day, they are antelopes. At first, they put a brave face on it and play the situation for laughs – they headbutt each other, bother smaller wildlife, and mock each other's antelope nobs. But as the sun sets, Daz (the player character, masterfully voiced by James Corden) begins to take the situation seriously. When the light drains from the sky, and the guttural roar of a lion rolls over the darkening plains, all the laughter is gone, and a very different game begins. From that night on, it's Daz's job to keep the lads alive in the wild until they can find a way to undo the curse. Just staying hydrated is hard enough, and the landscape itself is a killer – but the encounters with predators are *horrendous*. The game's first cheetah encounter was enough to make even the hardest souls jump out of their skins, and avoiding lions and hyenas by night was atavistically unpleasant. But all this horror served a purpose. Having become literal items of meat, the lads soon found the hollow dominance rituals they had used to shore up their self-esteem were useless – their only hope now lay in supporting, caring and looking out for each other. By the end of the first in-game week, they were changed men, and players found themselves rooting for the boys to make it back to society with the lessons they had learned.

VERDICT

Whether you learn empathy for the lads, or come to question your own ways, there's no way you can play *Bantelopes* and not come out a slightly better person.

"A LOVELESS PORTRAIT OF FIVE BRAYING TWATS ON A SAFARI HOLIDAY."

82 SUNDAY AFTERNOON DESPAIR SOLDIERS

SORROW SIM USING VARIOUS GLOOMY METAPHORS TO ILLUSTRATE THE DEATH OF THE WEEKEND.

YEAR
2013

GENRE
Sadness / Party Game

DEVELOPER
Liz Prompt

FORMAT
Nintendo Wii U

The chest-clenching sadness of Sunday afternoons might seem like a terrible theme for a game – and upon release, this grim offering from indie developer Liz Prompt seemed to support that conclusion. In *SADS* it was always February, and the sky was always as low and grey as a lead sheet. There were never any plans for the day, nor any way to avoid the looming prospect of spending five days doing something you hated in the name of making money for someone else. There was just the dismal stretch of hours between 9am, when you woke under sheets that badly needed changing, and midnight, when you gave up. The first phase of the game, the 'motivation phase,' allowed you to attempt various hobby projects by participating in frenzies of button mashing, but no matter how hard you tried, your thumbs always tired before anything much was achieved. Then it was onto the housework, where you attempted the tasks necessary to keep your life in a state of vague dignity, by completing touchscreen puzzles. This tended to go well at first, but as it went on you would become aware of more and more ravens perched on items of furniture, each cawing the word "why?" The more ravens present, the harder the puzzles got, until you finally snapped and chased them outside. There followed a segment where you trudged around your garden with a rake, using the Wii remote in fruitless attempts to swat them from the air. When it got dark you had to retreat to the house, where you could have another go at the motivation phase. This time, however, skeletal hounds would begin slinking in from the shadows, and you had to constantly break from your tasks to shoo them away. In time, the hounds became too numerous, and you were gradually pushed back to the bedroom, and then to bed, where they could not harm you. There, as the clock shuddered towards midnight, your only option was to press the sleep button, and bring the weekend to a weak end.

At first, players were baffled by *SADS* – sure, it was a solid artistic statement, but its futility made it a fairly shit game. Then, however someone discovered the hidden multiplayer mode. It turned out that not only were other players able to help with button mashing and puzzle minigames – they also had a huge stat boost when it came to swatting away ravens and dogs. It seemed the only way to beat the game (or at least come close) was to ask your friends for help.

VERDICT

A shrewd exploration of futility, dread, and smashing ravens with rakes.

"THERE WAS JUST THE DISMAL STRETCH OF HOURS BETWEEN 9AM, WHEN YOU WOKE UNDER SHEETS THAT BADLY NEEDED CHANGING, AND MIDNIGHT, WHEN YOU GAVE UP."

83 FIRST PERSON SHOOTER

PLAY A TIME TRAVELLER TREKKING ACROSS ANCIENT EAST AFRICA TO FIND, AND SHOOT, THE FIRST EVER PERSON.

YEAR
2014

GENRE
Time Travel / Survival

DEVELOPER
Ergaster Studios

FORMAT
PC, PlayStation 4,
Xbox One

You wake during a thunderstorm, up to your hips in the stormwaters of a tropical ravine. You can't remember what you were doing the night before, but a device on your wrist tells you it's more than 300,000 years in the past, and that you are in East Africa, so it must have been pretty heavy. You're wearing khaki fatigues, hiking boots, and a backpack containing a box of matches, a knife, and a lightweight sniper rifle with ten bullets. With no idea why you're there, your priority is survival: you must find shelter, build a fire, and last the night. When fatigue gets the better of you, your dreams come in the form of a strange briefing. Maps and diagrams flutter before you, and a robotic voice explains your purpose – to seek out, and put a bullet through, the first anatomically modern human, and thus the common ancestor of all living people. The target is some 100km from your location, however, and it's going to take ten days or more hiking up a primeval rift valley to get there. You are wished happy hunting, and *First Person Shooter* begins. For the most part, the game was a hardcore survival experience – during your epic trek up the valley, you faced challenges from pleistocene wildlife to extreme terrain, harsh weather, hunger, thirst and infections. But your biggest battle was with yourself. Each night upon making camp and settling down, further dream sequences would show possible backgrounds for your character: were you a ruthless billionaire hunting for the ultimate kill? An eco-terrorist trying to erase the whole of the anthropocene? Or a bioweapon created by a sentient AI and sent back to stop the human resistance, like a sort of better thought out version of the Terminator? It was never made quite clear, and it shrouded the game in uneasy mystery. But when players finally reached the area occupied by the first person's family group, things became even more mysterious, as it transpired the player *was also being hunted*, by a sniper clad in shimmering, ghostly camouflage. Without spoiling the game's legendary denouement, it's safe to say that *FPS*'s resolution did not go in the direction many players predicted.

VERDICT

While not always perfect in its presentation of hominid paleontology, *FPS* managed to be both a cripplingly tough survival experience, and a thoroughly compelling sci-fi mystery story.

"FOR THE MOST PART, THE GAME WAS A HARDCORE SURVIVAL EXPERIENCE."

84 YOU RANG?

UMPSCARE HORROR ABOUT SURVIVING THE NIGHT IN A MANSION FULL OF FERAL BUTLERS.

YEAR
2014

GENRE
Domestic Service /
Jumpscare Horror

DEVELOPER
Belvedere Software

FORMAT
Xbox One

In this preposterous horror game, you played as a luckless cretin who'd taken a job advertised in a local paper, looking for someone to watch over the home of a reclusive billionaire while they were out of town for a night. As the mansion's front gates slammed shut behind you at sunset, a timer would fade in at the top of the screen, counting down, in real-time, the minutes until dawn, when the master of the house would return to pay you $5,000 for your vigilance. It all sounded too good to be true – and, of course, it fucking was. As you entered the mansion itself, a voicemail from the absent billionaire would come in 'reminding you' to bring a shotgun to the job. You see, it transpired the newspaper ad had failed to mention a crucial fact about the mansion: that it was infested with hundreds of abhuman, ghoulish butlers. But not to worry, the voicemail added cheerfully, the butlers were perfectly reasonable servants, so long as the house remained brightly lit. That was, of course, the moment when the power cut out, the first ravenous screeches drifted up from the cellars, and the fun began. And oh, what fun. *You Rang?* wasn't a game that eased you into things lightly – within a minute of the lights going out, you would be set upon by a scrambling horror in an embroidered waistcoat, intent on gnawing your face off with its stinking fangs. You had to run fast, and keep running for however long it took to find something to fight the butler off with. If you ran into another grisly servant in the process, that was it – game over, or at least a heavy maiming. Once you'd bought yourself time to think, the plan of action for surviving the night was up to you – you could raid the gardener's premises for power tools to fight back with, search the kitchen for knives, or go in search of the house's generator to get some lights working again. Extremely brave players could even make it their mission to wipe out the butlers altogether, constructing an improvised flamethrower and descending into the wine cellars where the fiends had made their hive. Standard butlers become easier to deal with as player experience racked up, but Boss Butlers such as Greasy Jeeves, Big Smythe, and Pale Jenkins were always bad news if encountered without extensive prep.

VERDICT

Pitilessly hard, and merciless in its scare tactics, *You Rang?* took a hard bastard indeed to complete in one sitting, especially at night and with headphones on.

Sunrise in: 00:25:23

Warning

"YOU HAD TO RUN FAST, AND KEEP RUNNING FOR HOWEVER LONG IT TOOK TO FIND SOMETHING TO FIGHT THE BUTLER OFF WITH."

85 OPINION KING DEBATE ARENA

Barron-82: *But its proven already m8*

KEVIN-thaBoss: Show me the graphs then

SycElephant3: *Geddim, bawse!*

Everyone knows we evolv

TOOL FOR THOSE ADDICTED TO SOCIAL MEDIA ARGUMENTS, WHERE FEELINGS AND OPINIONS CAN BE VENTED INTO A FAKE UI POPULATED BY ADVANCED CHATBOTS.

YEAR
2014

GENRE
Meaningless Argument

DEVELOPER
Unknown

FORMAT
Web App

Some people just love arguing. For these poor sods, there is no pleasure greater than getting home, pouring themselves a carrier bag of wine, and going on the internet to roar at people. They patrol the digital wastes like jaded mercenaries after the collapse of a medieval war, looking for any sign of an opposing viewpoint, then laying into it with everything they've got. It's not about winning or losing for them – deep in their hearts, they know that nobody ever changed their mind because of an online pissing match. No: it's the raw, gladiatorial thrill of hollering your own beliefs over the top of someone else's that makes these folks tick. They are the people who get into nine-hundred-comment-deep feuds under YouTube videos of sausages cooking. They are the ones who think 'good morning' is an obvious jumping off point for a puce-faced rant about the virtues of capital punishment. They keep folders and folders full of links to dodgy graphs about immigration, and are the sort of people who use the word 'methinks' unironically. But despite it all, they see themselves as genteel debaters akin to the Greeks of Old, even while they're rupturing half the blood vessels in their face battering out 500 words in all caps about why women shouldn't be allowed to have jobs. Luckily, in 2014, some unknown saint gave us a way to contain them. *Opinion King Debate Arena* is an app which plugs into popular social media hell BookFace, and allows a user to generate several bots with which to engage in a good old barney. These bots can be customised to be anything from ragingly hostile to outright sycophantic, and have many other settings to play with besides – they can be serious or jocular, stubborn or pliable, and those who get a rush from pointing out mistakes in others' spelling and grammar can even set their linguistic ability. Most importantly, however, *they never tire*. They simply argue back for as long as required, locking the debate initiators into their own little nirvanas of endless discord, and letting the rest of us get on with our lives in peace.

VERDICT

While it stretched the definition of 'game' somewhat, this robotic sparring partner for gits was surely enough of a public service to deserve an honourable mention in this book.

bookface 🔍 Search on Facebook 🔍 👤 Kevin | Home ▾

Kevin

OpinionKiNG

Barron-82: *Yeah but don't u think they should fund science classes in schools tho?*

KEVIN-thaBoss: What makes u think £££ will go 2 schools??? methinks MPs will be 'requisitioning' this money to line they're own pockets!! An honest Politician? LOL! I would have better chances of finding a monkey giving birth to a human!!!

SycElephant3: *HA! So right* 😄

Gr0nd: *I say no money for these so called "evilution" scientists til they can prove It's not jsut a Theory!!!!*

Barron-82: *But its proven already m8*

KEVIN-thaBoss: Show me the graphs then

SycElephant3: *Geddim, bawse!*

-Barron-82
-SycElephant3
-Gr0nd

Everyone knows we evolved from pigs u cun

🎥 aA 🖼 😊 Send

Generate Debater

☐ Friendly
☐ Clever
☐ Understanding
☐ Listening
☐ Opponent
☐ Doubter
☐ Agreed
☐ Constructive

Generate

✏ Write your life | 🎞 Album Photos/Video

Yet Another DISGRACEFUL *LIE* from the "so called" experts at Oxford...

Post

Recent
2013
2012
2011
2010
2009
Born

"IT'S THE RAW, GLADIATORIAL THRILL OF HOLLERING YOUR OWN BELIEFS OVER THE TOP OF SOMEONE ELSE'S THAT MAKES THESE FOLKS TICK."

10 MIRACLES OF GAMING INNOVATION

Wild proliferation in device technology, along with an increasingly playful and experimental approach to game design, has led to many weird and wonderful developments in the last few years. Some used odd peripheral devices for output or input, while others mucked around with what players perceived of the world to create augmented realities. Others still involved players fucking massive papier-mâché yachts, but mainly that was *Yacht Fucker 6*, and we don't really want to talk about that any more. Anyway, where were we? Innovation. Yes, right. Read these:

01 YOU LOSE YOU SNOOZE // Swamp Kidz, 2014

An FPS arena duel with a powerful twist, *YLYS* gave players what you might call a shockingly good incentive to defeat their opposition. The reason you might call it that was because each player wore a locked iron mask, which would discharge a massive electric shock if their character reached 0 HP, knocking them out for a nice, hour-long nap. It almost probably didn't cause brain damage, but after three accidental deaths it was banned anyway.

02 DIGITAL SLEEPYBOY // Bungsleydale Novelties, 2015

This jaunty combination of console and alarm clock, which sat innocently on your bedside table like a child in a horror film concealing an axe, became the most hated consumer item of 2015. It would wake you at random hours in the night, alarm blaring, and would not let you rest again until you had completed an entire level of frantic, neon platform game action.

03 WARCAT // Runcible Entertainment, 2017

Unlike the last two hateful innovations, *WARCAT* was a genuine boon to mankind, using motion sensors to track the movement of a player's cat, then translating them onto a feline colossus made of stone in a fantasy battlefield environment. Using a jingly toy on a string, you could thus coax your mog into swiping aside whole platoons of goblins, or pouncing on a dwarven general with claws drawn.

04 WOLOLO! // Priestly Pursuits, 2016

In this blindingly simple augmented reality game, experienced via high-tech spectacles, players would wave their arms in the air and chant the name of the game in order to turn red things blue, and blue things red. Shit got real when two players encountered each other on the street.

05 PANIC ROWER // Electric Zeus, 201

Although the record for 'largest control device' is still held by 1992's *Ultra Car Driver*, which was in fact just a car marketed as a video game for tax reasons, *Panic Rower* comes close: it came with a full rowing machine as a peripheral, which it used to simulate sea monster chases, whale hunts, pirate battles and other stressful situations at sea. Faced with these nautical crises, players had little choice but to become immensely strong.

06 HROOP BLUPPER 9 // Flurply Bips, 2017

Wamulo! In this grombly old borgler of a game, you had to blup a series of increasingly gurning hroops without totally glopping your blap. Harder than it sounds, especially when you set borps to sluppery, and glepped all five bluppers to activate muppo mode.

07 CIGARETTES: THE GAME // Marlboro, 2015

While this tablet and mobile app was free to download, each time you opened its matte black icon, 50p would be removed from your bank account. Once you were in, you simply watched a loading bar diminish over the course of six minutes, while developing a mild headache. It was almost as fun as the real thing, but somehow lacked the element of danger.

08 THE FRIDGE // Code Knights, 2017

The Fridge was a fairly traditional dungeon crawler, pitting you against farting bats, fat ants and all the other classic fantasy staples, but it had a twist: it was connected via bluetooth to olfactory sensors in your fridge. The more rotten food the sensors detected, the more the game would cheat in favour of the monsters when it came to virtual dice rolls.

09 OUTLOOK TOILHOUND // Whispersmith Solutions, 2016

Supposedly designed to promote good working habits, this concrete dog peripheral would connect to your email client, then sit on your desk glowering and reading out your mail in an accusatory whisper until you did something about it. Every single one ended up thrown in the sea.

10 CYCLE OF VIOLENCE // Dog Haiku Games, 2013

A clever little mobile game that could be hooked up to compatible exercise bikes, and displayed a simple side-scrolling beat-'em-up. The revs per minute generated by the player would determine the rate of forward motion, punch power and general level of aggression of the tiny martial artist onscreen.

86 TRISTRAM SHANDY ONLINE

INFURIATING RPG, WITH A NOTORIOUSLY CONVOLUTED CHARACTER CREATION PROCESS FROM WHICH FEW PLAYERS HAVE EVER ESCAPED.

YEAR
2015

GENRE
Digression / RPG

DEVELOPER
Yorick Studios

FORMAT
PC

Despite being completely free to play, and apparently quite fun, only a handful of people populate the servers of *Tristram Shandy Online*, and they refuse to tell the rest of the world what goes on there. That's because the real challenge in this game, one that has confounded millions of prospective players in the years since its release, is the navigation of its mammoth character creation tool. On first loading, it seems incredibly simple and clearly laid out – you must select an interesting fact about your character's backstory, customise a few basic aspects of their appearance, and then choose a couple of special skills. It looks like it'll take a couple of minutes tops. But then the first mouse click drops – and the dialog boxes start popping up. Three hours later, you're weeping in frustration as you choose a playlist of French folk music for another player to listen to while they draw a portrait of the woman your great-great-grandfather fell in love with, in the hopes that once they have done so, you will be able to unlock the next personality quiz based on your interpretation of the destruction of the library in chapter six of *Don Quixote*. It can take hundreds of hours of gameplay to even reach the appearance customisation options, and even then you can't proceed until you've correctly answered two hundred questions on the game's suggested reading list of essays on the philosophical significance of different types of noses. It's not all study and toil – one branch of the fifteenth section of the background selection process can unlock a full-length point-and-click adventure in which two retired military men get into various scrapes while trying to recreate famous battles in miniature. But even then, play stops for frequent flashbacks conducted through branching narrative exercises, and when one of these sidelines you into a character creation process for a nameless French soldier mentioned in passing, it can be very tempting to scream until you die. But if you eventually want to start playing *Tristram Shandy Online*, there's no option but to press on.

VERDICT

The only way to cope with the character creation process in *TSO* is to forget the hope it might one day lead to something better, and just enjoy it for what it is. Bit like life, really.

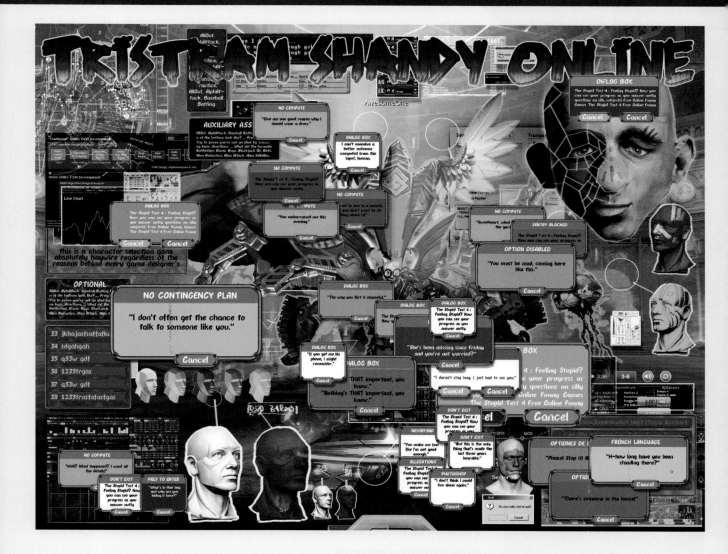

"IT CAN BE VERY TEMPTING TO SCREAM UNTIL YOU DIE."

87

SUNHURL BINSHOUT

SPD 51MPH

SUBLIMELY EFFECTIVE, KEYBOARD-CONTROLLED MICROGAME IN WHICH A LUMPEN OAF HURLS BINS AT THE SUN WITH A DIGITAL YODEL.

YEAR
2015

GENRE
Letting It All Out / Throwing Bins

DEVELOPER
Thunderswan Interactive

FORMAT
Web game

In some ways, this game was the dark reflection of 2008's seminal *Vin Diesel's Weasel Easel* (p. 164) – while that game soothed away the crushing burden of modernity by putting you under the caring aegis of a cinema strongman, this title goaded you into revelling in your frustration and using it to hurl bins at the sun. Your in-game avatar was a sweating goliath with hands the size of dogs and an expression of baffled anguish etched permanently on his face. After selecting a bin from a stinking row, he would seize it in his industrial-sized mitts and begin dragging it across the dying grass. His pace would increase as you smacked at the keyboard, flat feet slapping at the ground with the increasing tempo of your keystrokes. The wind would whistle, the bin would rise from the ground, and the giant's chest would begin to swell with the beginnings of a mighty shout. Then, when the landscape began rushing past in a blur, you would batter the space bar, and the bin would fly. With the shout of release still echoing, the camera would follow the hurtling canister as it escaped the atmosphere and – if the throw had been good enough – plunged straight into the photosphere of the sun with a satisfying *WHOOSH*. Even a poor shot had a good chance of clanging aggressively into the moon, while a truly duff throw would still likely brain a truck or shatter a plate glass window a few miles away. No matter how you performed, it just felt really good to be able to throw a bin into the sky with a honk of profound, if shapeless, emotion.

After the astonishing success of the original *Sunhurl*, developers Thunderswan Interactive wasted no time taking the formula to the next level with the funds they had accrued. So was born *Anvilhurl Catharsis*, in which you could briefly cast free the cloying madness of urban life using a VR headset, a pair of lead mittens, and a soundproofed astronaut helmet. Sure, anyone playing the game was almost guaranteed to smash up their living room in the process, but as sales figures testified, this was apparently a small price to pay.

VERDICT

While primal scream therapy is one of the more heavily discredited schools of psychiatry, clinical trials have yet to assess the efficacy of *Sunhurl Binshout*. We reckon it could be an absolute gamechanger in the field.

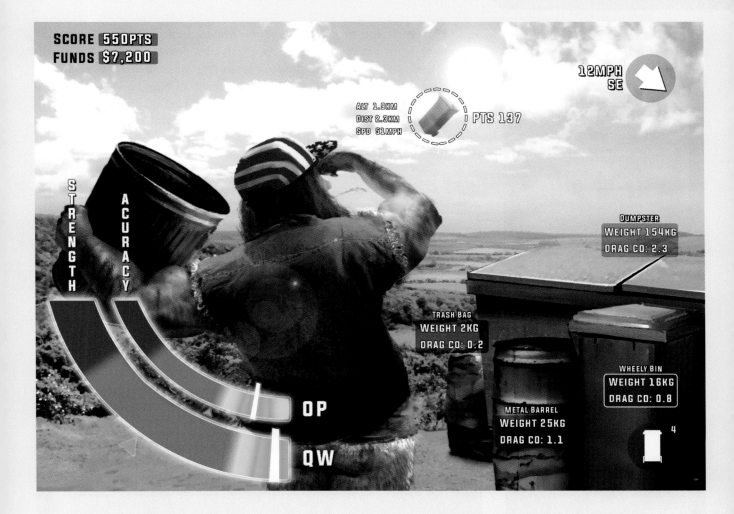

SCORE **550PTS**
FUNDS **$7,200**

12MPH
SE

ALT 1.9KM
DIST 2.3KM
SPD 51MPH
PTS 137

STRENGTH

ACURACY

OP

QW

DUMPSTER
WEIGHT 154KG
DRAG CO: 2.3

TRASH BAG
WEIGHT 2KG
DRAG CO: 0.2

WHEELY BIN
WEIGHT 16KG
DRAG CO: 0.8

METAL BARREL
WEIGHT 25KG
DRAG CO: 1.1

4

"EVEN A POOR SHOT HAD A GOOD CHANCE OF CLANGING AGGRESSIVELY INTO THE MOON."

88 GENGHIS CAN'T

RETELLING OF THE FAMED WARLORD'S STORY WHERE HE SUFFERS FROM ABYSSAL SELF-BELIEF & YOU MUST GIVE HIM THE ENCOURAGEMENT HE NEEDS TO CONQUER EURASIA.

YEAR
2015

GENRE
Mental Health / Grand Strategy

DEVELOPER
School Assembly

FORMAT
PC

Even historians tend to imagine Genghis Khan, possibly the most successful conqueror in the history of mankind, as a fairly confident bloke. The logic seems reasonable; one doesn't tend to unite the warring tribes of the endless steppe and sweep across an entire continent in a tsunami of blood and steel without a *little* bit of swagger to you. Nevertheless, with almost no first-hand accounts of the man having survived to the present day (presumably due to the subject's famously cavalier approach to burning things), it's impossible to be certain of his character. Enter developers School Assembly, who reimagined the Great Khan as an uncertain, melancholy figure in their grand strategy epic, *Genghis Can't*. Unlike most games of its type, *GC* was less about marshalling and applying military force, and more about building up the confidence required to do so. Much of the game was spent asking your advisers whether they really thought you were good at war, or whether they were just saying it to cheer you up, while campaigning often paused so you could spend glum days in the countryside with your pet eagle Garid, trying to shake off the blues. In time, Genghis' gloom would spread to his troops too – by the invasion of Central Asia in the 1220s, despite enjoying numerical superiority over nearly all foes, the Khan's armies were often just too miserable to get the job done, prompting the player to engage in a tricky balancing act between buoying up their own sense of self-worth, and the collective mood of their soldiers.

While it seemed like an original concept to many, *Genghis Can't* was – by the admission of its own devs – intended as a spiritual successor to 1992's *Sighborg*. This game, now almost forgotten, featured a war machine created by humans to fight off an overwhelming alien invasion, but too deeply depressed to really care about doing so. Playing as an army psychotherapist, you had to convince the steel titan to love itself enough to get on with the defence of the earth, while avoiding succumbing to its incredibly negative worldview yourself.

VERDICT

While history leaves no doubt that Genghis Khan was a genocidal sociopath on par with the worst the 20th Century had to offer, it's hard not to feel just a bit sorry for him when playing *Genghis Can't*.

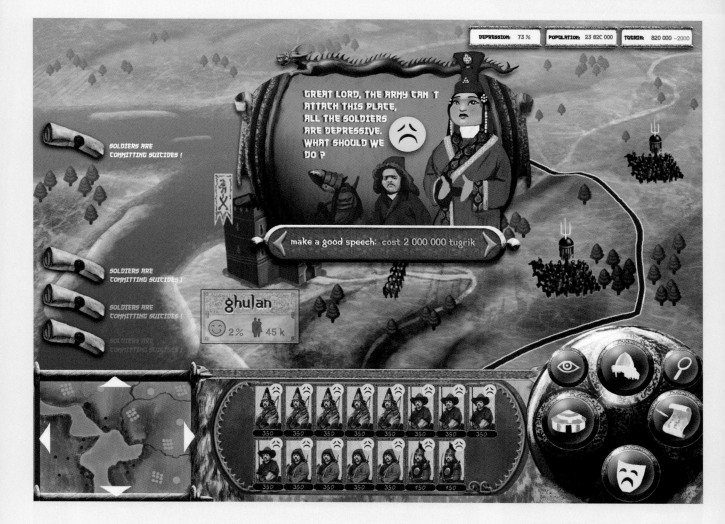

"MUCH OF THE GAME WAS SPENT ASKING YOUR ADVISERS WHETHER THEY REALLY THOUGHT YOU WERE GOOD AT WAR."

89 BREAD: THE GAME

MULTI-GENRE EXTRAVAGANZA CELEBRATING THE RICH HISTORY OF THE WHEATY TREAT.

YEAR
2016

GENRE
Roll-Playing Game

DEVELOPER
The British League of Bakers

FORMAT
Xbox One, PlayStation 4, Nintendo 3DS

Bread: it's just a staple food prepared by baking a dough of milled cereals and water, right? Wrong. It's a fucking phenomenon. And while games have touched on the theme before (notably 1994's mafia sandwich shop comedy *Baguette About It,* and 2003's horror title *House of Pain* with its grim human-loaf hybrids), no developer had been brave enough to give bread the game it deserved until the British League of Bakers funded this production in 2016. And they didn't half-arse the job, either. When asked by the design team what genre of game they wanted their pet project to be, the president of the League famously replied "All of them," before eating a whole tiger loaf in a single, mighty gulp. And so that's what they got: *B:TG* takes players through a tour de force not just of the history of bread, but of the wide variety of play styles honed during the last forty years of games development. The result, it's fair to say, was the toast of the town.

The ten distinct phases of *Bread: The Game:*

Dawn of the Bread: Text adventure telling the story of bread's discovery in 30,000BC.

No Pain, No Grain: Strategy game demonstrating the advantage conferred to early civilisations by developing an agricultural economy focused around the production of bread.

Duty and the Yeast: Shooter somehow managing to describe the discovery of leavened bread.

Loafing Around: Lighthearted platformer about a medieval baker.

The Slice is Right: Madcap racer celebrating the euphoric advent of sliced bread.

Earl-y Days: RPG featuring the Earl of Sandwich, and culminating in the dramatic invention of the great man's namesake during an intense round of simulated poker.

Breadwinner: Fighting game where a man made of bread defeats other cereal-based foods.

Having Naan Of It: Quiz game evaluating various global bread types, before (perhaps unfairly) declaring the classic wheat loaf the undisputed winner.

Dough and Behold: Management game where players use the Chorleywood process to drastically improve efficiencies during the mass production of bread.

Sarniegeddon: Fast-paced rhythm game celebrating perennial lunch favourite sandwiches.

VERDICT

The best thing since sliced bread.

PLAYER UPGRADE
■ BREAD TYPE
■ FILLING
■ TOPPING

CINNAMON PRETZEL
TONGUE-TWISTING TASTE

LA BAGUET
WELCOME TO F

SEEDED BAGEL
HIPSTER-STYLE

SLICE!

"WIDE VARIETY
OF PLAY STYLES
HONED DURING
THE LAST FORTY
YEARS OF GAMES
DEVELOPMENT."

9∅ WAR, ON DRUGS

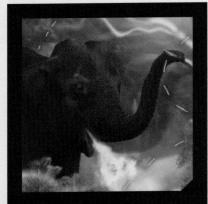

BRAINMASHING VR EXPERIENCE; WITNESS CONFLICTS THROUGHOUT HISTORY WHILE UNDER THE SIMULATED INFLUENCE OF A WIDE VARIETY OF NARCOTICS.

YEAR
2016

GENRE
Being Mashed / FPS

DEVELOPER
Digital Shaman

FORMAT
HTC Vive

From the mushroom-chomping berserkers of Icelandic saga to the permastoned troopers of the Vietnam War, there has always been a strong narrative association between drugs and war. Of course, it may have been that the Norse berserkers were just men who were very cross, and the prevalence of drug use in Vietnam is a thorny topic bound up in the politics of Nixon-era America. But hey, why let the truth get in the way of a good first person shooter? Because let's be honest, while it certainly wasn't the most morally responsible title ever burnt to disc, *War, On Drugs* was – as they* say – a total banger. After slapping on your VR headset, you simply chose your war, chose what drugs you wanted to experience it on, and got cracking. You could be historically accurate (getting through Trafalgar on a pint of rum was a riot every time), or you could go freestyle: taking a Spartan through Thermopylae on a high-octane blend of speed and ketamine was mind-altering in itself, while the 1187 AD siege of Jerusalem was a hell of a thing to get through on acid. The techniques with which the game simulated being narco-battered were as creative as they were varied, ranging from audiovisual distortion filters to control modifiers which could make head movements translate to nauseatingly slow drifts, glitchy snaps, or wild swings in the wrong direction. The UI was also prone to alteration; for example, even a mild virtual noseful of blow would make all of your stats display at several times their real values, while enough weed would turn your health meter into a bag of crisps that grew larger and larger until it eclipsed most of the screen, and would only disappear once a bag of crisps had been found and consumed. This was not terribly helpful when it happened during a pitched mace duel. And that was the thing about this game: while pretty much everything you could choose to ingest made battles more interesting, very little of it actually made you any better at war. Because after all, you know what they say – winners don't do drugs.

*Drugs guys.

VERDICT

While some might question *WOD* as a premise, few could go through Gettysburg on MDMA and then deny the quality of the project's execution.

"YOU SIMPLY CHOSE YOUR WAR, CHOSE WHAT DRUGS YOU WANTED TO EXPERIENCE IT ON, AND GOT CRACKING."

10 VIRTUALLY REAL VIRTUAL REALITY GAMES

After a few awkward false starts in decades past, it seems that Virtual Reality – essentially strapping a small telly to your face – is here to stay. With several dedicated VR consoles now at large on the market, VR games have gone from being one-trick novelties to full-on game experiences, complete with incredibly advanced naturalistic control methods. Here are ten of the sharpest around:

01 SPIN DOCTORS // Didgeridon't, 2016

This nausea-inducing hospital experience puts you in the shoes of an emergency doctor in an Accident & Emergency department on a Saturday night, and challenges you to treat patients' injuries while your point of view constantly rotates. Enjoy doing stitches, champ.

02 TOUCAN PLAY THAT GAME // Soft Conker Entertainment, 2017

This adorable game allows two pals to play as a pair of toucans, wearing headsets with special beak attachments to interact with the game. The two colourful birds are charged with finding an appropriate tree hollow to make a home in, then setting up a lovely nest and doing some eggs.

03 GREENLAND SHARK // Lemniscatic Studios, Forthcoming

In this ultra-grim VR hellscape based on the shark of the same name, you play a 500-year-old macropredator on the hunt for rotting meat in a twilit ocean beneath a grinding expanse of ice. Decapod parasites blind you as play continues, meaning you must eventually resort to hunting by smell, represented by strange bloom graphics on the headset display.

04 PISS WARS // Fat Cowboy Games, Forthcoming

In this puerile military fantasy RTS, you generate resources for your faction by pissing in an actual bucket with an electronic measuring stick in it. You can't even cheat by pouring water in – this game will only settle for the taste of wee. If somehow this leaves you with any dignity, you can always tackle the "Whizzdrake" minigame, where your stream of wee is motion captured as a dragon's molten breath as it swoops over the enemy citadel. Pathetic.

05 PAT-A-CAKE WITH IDRIS ELBA // Unknown, 2017

This game does exactly what you would imagine it does: allows you to play schoolyard rhythm game Pat-a-Cake with the world's suavest actor, as he stares into your eyes & intones the song's traditional words in a voice like burnt sugar. We don't know who made it, but it's definitely Idris playing himself. As relaxing as it is perplexing.

06 CRAMPROOM CATSWING // BumBum Solutions, 2016

The app that nearly crashed the London property market. This ingenious piece of software links to property websites and allows you to swing various sizes of cat within the houses advertised, thereby allowing you to determine the actual size of rooms beyond the trick photography.

07 CHECKOUT // Big Night Out Games, 2016

This photorealistic simulation of a supermarket checkout challenged you with maintaining speed and accuracy, while spotting the occasional shapeshifting monsters coming down the conveyor disguised as groceries. If the beasts entered the bagging area as unexpected items, they would transform, turning the game very rapidly into a close combat simulator.

08 WEEEEEE! // Numbergrowl, Forthcoming

Putting aside all the injuries, sharks and piss, this wonderful little game harnesses the power of VR for pure childlike fun. All you do is climb an enchanted tower, then chuck pancakes off the top and follow their progress as they spiral down to the bustling streets below.

09 DANGERWANK // Spafftech, 2017

Embarassingly crude adult title supporting multiple genital configurations; gameplay was simply a matter of getting the job done before you got busted, in environments including the Houses of Parliament, a cretaceous forest and the battle of Stalingrad.

10 GLOOMSTUB HOTSPLASH // Rough Ronalds, 2016

A brutally realist simulation of carrying a mug of piping hot tea across a dark room strewn with lego, while nursing a savage hangover. Came with special shoe peripherals that were studded with needlessly powerful electrodes.

91 BINCRAB DESTINY

DREARY AUGMENTED REALITY PET COLLECTION APP WHERE THE ONLY CREATURES AVAILABLE ARE SURLY, BIN-DWELLING CRABS.

YEAR
2016

GENRE
Grubby Crustaceans /
Augmented Reality

DEVELOPER
Nantucket Studios

FORMAT
Mobile, Tablet

After augmented reality game *Monsterfind Wahey!* became the surprise hit of the summer of 2016, countless developers launched new projects to capitalise on the craze. Some were more flagrant than others, however, and San Francisco-based Nantucket Studios would become infamous for the most transparent 'me-too' product of them all. Originally titled *Pocketbeast Safari*, it was almost a direct copy of *Monsterfind*, and was intended for launch just three months after the game which had 'inspired' it. Of course, the hubris of this timescale soon bit hard – resource constraints and technical issues meant that when the big day came around, the game had barely a fraction of its planned feature list in place. Nevertheless, Nantucket's president Terry Hosepipe was anxious that any further delay could risk missing the AR pet-collection craze altogether, and so ordered it launched on time regardless of any shortcomings. The dev team balked, as their embryonic app's only functioning 'pet' was a loathsome crab, and the only real-world locations it had access to were public bins, but Hosepipe didn't give a hoot – the game would just have to go to market as it was. And so *BinCrab Destiny* was launched, to a world that was already largely sick of looking for monsters in alleyways. But despite a series of mocking editorials when the gaming press cottoned on to this tragic new arrival, what happened next surprised everyone – including Hosepipe. In a youth culture entirely suffused with jaded irony, it turned out a surprising number of people identified with miserable crabs who lurked in bins, and *BinCrab Destiny* was a smash hit. Something about it just seized the zeitgeist like a pair of mucky pincers around the slimy stem of a discarded banana peel, and download figures shot through the roof. Not only did it create as big a splash as *Monsterfind* had done, it proved to have more staying power – at the time of writing, *BinCrab*'s user base was up 7% year-on-year thanks to the recent release of the *Claws for Concern* creature pack, while the upcoming *Garbage Prawn Arena* update is expected to bring in even more new players.

VERDICT

BinCrab's runaway success may not have been expected, or entirely deserved, but it remains a great underdog story, if one where the dog has eyestalks and hides under a bin lid.

"SOMETHING ABOUT IT JUST SEIZED THE ZEITGEIST LIKE A PAIR OF MUCKY PINCERS AROUND THE SLIMY STEM OF A DISCARDED BANANA PEEL."

92

JAMES BONG 2: LICENSE TO CHILL

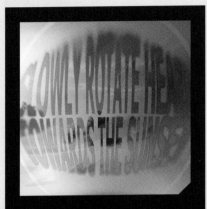

COMATOSE SEQUEL TO THE SEDATE CLASSIC: IN THIS INSTALLMENT, JAMES MUST TURN HIS HEAD SLIGHTLY IN ORDER TO WITNESS A SUNSET.

YEAR
2017

GENRE
Being Extremely High / Very Slight Head Movements

DEVELOPER
Blunt Instrument

FORMAT
PlayStation VR, PC

While the original *James Bong* raised eyebrows with its combination of spy adventure and off-beat stoner humour, it was at least still recognisable as a game of some sort. While true fans of the series probably won't remember the original's premise, it was clear enough – to stare at a poster of Bob Marley until it gave you a secret mission to buy nine bags of crisps, which you would then undertake. The simulation of handling a transaction with a newsagent during the nadir of a psychedelic journey was surprisingly stressful, but it all came good in the end, as James ate his crisps on the slow, colourful walk home (there was possibly a sequence with Russians on skis, too, but nobody is sure whether they dreamed that bit or not). The sequel, *License to Chill*, was considerably more abstract, as it continued James' mental odyssey into a place where most ordinary mortals were unable to follow. In this experience, best undertaken in VR, the player's only task was to turn their head ever so slightly over the course of an hour and a half, so as to bring a sunset into view. This was an incredibly pretty thing to witness, enhanced considerably by the floaty, prog-styled reworking of the *James Bond* theme which played throughout – but it was very hard to get into outside the mental state of the protagonist, and even harder to call a game. Still, with *James Bong: Moonbaker* coming out next year (and rumoured to be even less challenging than *License*), the series is clearly doing it for some people, so who are we to doubt the phenomenon?

While the *James Bong* series is developer Blunt Instrument's flagship franchise, it is probably worth mentioning their impressively committed, if thematically repetitive, back catalogue. After the release of soporific platformer *Chronic the Spliffhog* in 2004, they were best known for *Stonan the Barbarian*, an open world fantasy RPG which largely focused around buying and consuming crisps. Then came a foray into the westerns with 2008's *High Noon*, followed by sequel *High Plains Bifter*, before finally settling into the *James Bong* franchise in 2012. We'll say one thing for those guys – they sure do know what they like in life.

VERDICT

It's a pretty simple business, really – either *License to Chill* was your sort of thing, or it wasn't. And if it was, it was about as relaxing a game as a person could ask for.

"THE PLAYER'S ONLY TASK WAS TO TURN THEIR HEAD EVER SO SLIGHTLY OVER THE COURSE OF AN HOUR AND A HALF, SO AS TO BRING A SUNSET INTO VIEW."

93 MOTORWAY SPRINTER

WHIMSICAL AR TREAT; LOOK OUT OF A CAR WINDOW AND USE EYE MOVEMENT TO CONTROL A TINY PERSON HOPPING OVER PASSING CARS.

YEAR
2017

GENRE
Augmented Reality

DEVELOPER
Actual Wizard Labs

FORMAT
Sprintvision Zoomgoggles

Cast your mind back to long car journeys you took as a child, and imagine looking out of the window at the motorway as it sped past in a blur. The odds are, at some point, you imagined a tiny figure legging it along the road at incredible speeds, leaping cars and skidding down the length of metal barriers in synchronicity with the movement of your eyes. Heck, maybe you're still lucky enough to do this as an adult. Either way, if this rings a bell, then you are part of the astonishingly large target market for *Motorway Sprinter*. This game basically validated the concept of augmented reality all by itself, simply by addressing this phenomenon. Built into a pair of goggles, it allowed passengers to will a simple stick figure into existence beside the vehicle they were travelling in, and begin a marvellous steeplechase. Sensors tracked eyeball movement with astonishing precision, so that play could be controlled using the eyes alone, while winks, blinks and double blinks could be used in lieu of button presses. The object of the game was to collect coins, which the game would generate on top of the physical landscape. Once you had collected enough, a long blink would transform your character into a more advanced hero with special skills, including an ape who could swing between lamp posts, a skateboarding robot who threw up showers of sparks, and a hunchbacked pirate with a grappling hook. There was no real endgame, but that didn't matter – it was genuinely hypnotic to play, and could make even the longest journey pass without a dull moment. And with an update in the works to make *Motorway Sprinter* compatible with train travel, plus a rumoured sequel called *Cloud Racers* for use aboard aircraft, it seems the fun isn't due to end any time soon.

VERDICT

Motorway Sprinter wasn't just a cool gadget: it was an experience that spoke to a fundamental commonality of perception among modern humans. As Voltaire might have said if he had been a games journalist in 2017, "Si *Motorway Sprinter* n'existait pas, il faudrait l'inventer" – *If Motorway Sprinter did not exist, it would have to be invented.* Luckily for us all, however, someone did invent this game. Because just *imagine* the disappointment of finding you lived in a world without it.

"PLAY COULD BE CONTROLLED USING THE EYES ALONE, WHILE WINKS, BLINKS AND DOUBLE BLINKS COULD BE USED IN LIEU OF BUTTON PRESSES."

94 FRATBOY ANGELS

ST MICHAEL LEADS THE ANGELIC HOST TO WAR WITH A DEAFENING BLAST OF AIR HORNS AND REVVING TRUCK ENGINES IN THIS ULTRA-HIGH BUDGET, MULTI-PLATFORM SHITSHOW.

YEAR
2017

GENRE
Abrahamic Cosmology / Bros / Squad-Based Shooter

DEVELOPER
Sick Games, Bruh

FORMAT
Xbox One, PlayStation 4, PC

This game is a rare example of a concept so stupid it was offensive, but which came within a hair's breadth of redeeming itself by somehow turning the stupidity, and the production budget, up yet another notch. If it wasn't already clear from the game's iconic box art, and assuming you were in the blessed relief of a coma during the all-consuming marketing blitz that preceded its launch, this was a game about angels who were fratboys. Or fratboys who were angels. Or, to be more precise, about an intellectually bankrupt reworking of Abrahamic cosmology where the two concepts were merged for the sake of having burning swords and Uzis in the same game. There really wasn't much of a backstory to grasp. What narrative it did possess was a retelling of the war in Heaven, although whether this was the primeval struggle described by Milton or an eschatological vision of the end of time was – once again – perhaps too fine a theological issue to have troubled developers Sick Games, Bruh. The point was, there was a big fight between angels and devils, you played as the goodies, and that was enough to satisfy most of the target audience. The game allowed several good bros to play together via online co-op, with players taking on the roles of five powerful angels. Archangel Michael, leader of the heavenly host, was the damage dealer, while Gabriel, his keg-chugging best bud, was the tank of the team. Jophiel (The archangel of wisdom and understanding, and a cabalistic guardian of the Torah, according to the pseudepigraphical *Revelation of Moses*) was the spellcaster, and Raphael the laid-back, fun-loving healer. Then there was Metatron, the Chancellor of Heaven, who could change into a jeep because – to quote Sick Games, Bruh's lead developer Chad Dudesley, "His name sounded cool, kinda like a Transformer, you know?" There were beers, and guns, and holy reggaeton air horns which would summon hosts of angelic warriors when sounded. There were also way more Total Babes than seemed remotely sensitive to either the source material or the more general struggle against ingrained misogyny in gaming, but there you go. That was *Fratboy Angels*.

VERDICT

Imagining this game transported through time and into the hands of a group of medieval religious scholars is either really hilarious, or a bit depressing. Times have changed.

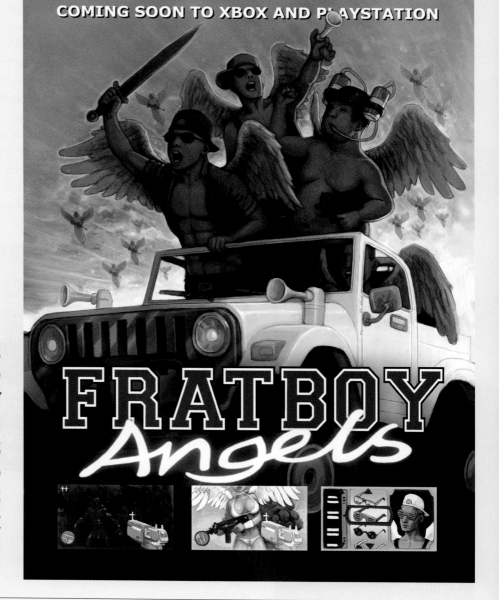

"THERE WERE BEERS, AND GUNS, AND HOLY REGGAETON AIR HORNS WHICH WOULD SUMMON HOSTS OF ANGELIC WARRIORS WHEN SOUNDED."

95 TUBA HERO

PLAY ALONG WITH EIGHTEEN HOURS OF OOMPAH CLASSICS BY ROARING INTO A TRAFFIC CONE ATTACHED TO YOUR CONSOLE WITH A FUCKING HOSE.

YEAR
2017

GENRE
'Music'

DEVELOPER
Lederhosen Games

FORMAT
PlayStation 4

Not so much a game as an existential ordeal, *Tuba Hero* demanded a pair of lungs like a leaf blower, no neighbours, and a completely broken understanding of the concept of fun. What the game's box described as a 'sophisticated tuba peripheral' was in fact a traffic cone taped to a hosepipe, which you jammed into the back of your console and bellowed into in order to 'play along' with an exhaustive collection of raucous Bavarian oompah tunes. There was no reward for keeping to the rhythm or the tune, nor indeed any hint that the game knew or cared what you were doing. You were just shouting into a traffic cone in an empty room, while your TV played deafeningly loud tuba music. If you bought this game, you might as well have gone all the way on your journey to ruin by burning down your house and playing it in the street. At least that way, you might have solicited a measure of pity and a handful of loose change from passers by.

A selection of other dire music games from Lederhosen:

Kazoo God 9: Latest in the interminable series; scream along to whatever mediocre 70s rock tunes the publishers could afford this time, using a shitty plastic kazoo on a string.

Comb and Paper Warrior: Pretty much the same as Kazoo God, but the peripheral is just a comb with a rizla folded over it, and the only song available is the *Benny Hill* theme.

Bin Lid Maestro: You've got a metal bin lid and a wooden spoon, but there's no music at all. You just smash away like a chimp having a crisis, and try to imagine you're playing a game.

Orchestra of Fools: Enterprising multipack containing all of the above. Buying this for a relative's children was essentially a declaration of war.

VERDICT

While *Tuba Hero* had precisely zero merit as a video game, the fact that its developers managed to convince people to pay £90 for a traffic cone, a length of hose and a CD of demented beerhall music was a triumph of modern marketing.

"TUBA HERO DEMANDED A PAIR OF LUNGS LIKE A LEAF BLOWER, NO NEIGHBOURS, AND A COMPLETELY BROKEN UNDERSTANDING OF THE CONCEPT OF FUN."

THE STATHAM PROBLEM

In its mission to chronicle the most iconic video games of the last 40 years, this book has so far made one problematic omission: games about Jason Statham. While many games about the shovel-chinned Lord of Action have been poor or even forgettable, one simply cannot write any sort of history of the medium without somehow tackling this vast oeuvre. There is just something about this elemental force of a man, whose head resembles an egg crossed with the concept of a fight, which has captured the imagination of games designers since the dawn of the industry.

Indeed, it has now come to light that the first game to feature Jason Statham was created *before the man himself*. In the summer of 1967, television engineer Ralph Baer created the very first, primitive games console – a simple wooden creation called TV Game Unit #7, or the 'Brown Box.' Its main game, *Pursuit*, was a simple affair where two dots could chase each other around a screen. But recent examination of a prototype held in the Smithsonian museum has revealed the Brown Box had a second, hidden game. Simply titled *He Comes*, it featured only a blank screen, which flashed once when the controls were touched.

Jason Statham was born on 26th July, 1967, the same day as this prototype was activated for the first time.

After that mysterious incident, Statham was absent from the history of games for some time. There are plenty of urban legends about his appearance in games during the 1980s, but these have all emerged recently, and are largely considered to be artefacts of modern hysteria. For example, many now swear that if one flew far enough away from the play area in 1985's *Helicopter Squad*, a vast figure resembling Statham would rise from the sand to consume the player's aircraft, but this is yet to be verified with undoctored game footage.

Still, from the early 1990s onwards, and particularly following his film debut as 'Bacon' in 1998's *Lock, Stock and Two Smoking Barrels*, the Stath became a near ubiquitous figure in the field of game design. In 1993, he featured as the antagonist in dungeon adventure *Stabyrinth*, where he lurked at the heart of the game's maze with a Stanley knife, while 1995 saw the release of *Super Statham* for the Super Nintendo, in which you hammered the controller's yellow button to make him run faster and faster towards the screen until your heart gave up in fear.

PC games gave the living threat plenty of airtime too, with 1997's *Inner Statham* portraying him as a doctor who treated patients by shrinking himself and beating the shit out of viruses, and 1999's *Rubik's Cube with Jason Statham* offering a fairly straightlaced simulation of the classic puzzle in which Jason would occasionally help the player by threatening squares into changing colour. The same year also saw the release of *Stathamagotchi*, a virtual pet toy which contained an LCD representation of the film star, in a state of total apoplexy due to his imprisonment in a small plastic egg.

The 2000s were rife with portrayals of Statham: the *Fyst* series of mystery games chronicled his struggle to understand and master the concept of rage while trapped on an enigmatic island, while the marvellous *Jason*

Statham's Art Attack featured his mystical quest to climb into every painting in the National Gallery in order to fight their occupants. In 2008, the release of *Aliens vs Statham* kickstarted the star's long-running association with Ridley Scott's beloved sci-fi franchise, which most recently culminated in the 2015 survival horror blockbuster *Statham: Isolation*.

In recent years, representations of the Punch King have proliferated into every conceivable genre and platform. The 2013 mobile game *Flappy Statham* starred a small cartoon version of Jason, hurtling through a wilderness of pipes with his arms windmilling angrily to keep him aloft, while *Jason Statham's VR Tarot* was a 2016 fortune telling sim, in which every card bore his face and prompted a terrifying chase sequence. Meanwhile, controversy was courted with the release of *StathNav*, a seemingly harmless navigation app for drivers which, in the summer of 2017, began posing riddles in Statham's voice, and steering people's cars into ditches if they couldn't answer quickly enough.

Perhaps fittingly, the most recent addition to the proud history of games about Jason Statham is the means by which all previous games can be remade in his image. Known as the Game Statham, this mysterious device – which projects into our reality as a small plastic model of the man's head – can be affixed to any console in order to make Jason Statham a controllable character in whatever game is being played at the time. While we do not yet know what dark price the advent of the Game Statham may exact upon humanity, we do not imagine it could ever be too much to pay for the privilege it has given us.

96 REVERSE JUMANJI

PLAY A GORILLA PROTECTING HER FAMILY AS A HAUNTED SMARTPHONE CONJURES MARKETING PLANS AND SPREADSHEETS INTO HER JUNGLE HOME.

YEAR
2017

GENRE
Metaphors for Urban Anxiety / Action-Adventure

DEVELOPER
Clappenhoot Enterprises

FORMAT
Smartphone

Sometimes, you don't need many words to tell a good story. Indeed, the intro cutscene to *Reverse Jumanji* is perfect without any at all. Set in the heart of a Ugandan forest, it introduces us to a nameless female mountain gorilla, foraging for food with her young son. When she notices the small ape is missing, she leaves the family group to search for him, and finds him in a nearby clearing, investigating the body of a marketing consultant. She tries to coax him away, but it is no use – the inquisitive youngster has fished a smartphone from the dead executive's pocket, and is staring, entranced, at the apps it contains. A terrible rumbling fills the air, and we see the leathery finger of the baby gorilla in close up, as it touches a tickbox and consents to a user agreement. The mother screams in warning, but it's too late – her baby is sucked into the phone, and it zooms off into the forest in an explosion of printouts, spreadsheets and KPIs. From that point on you were dumped straight into the action, as the gorilla began a hectic chase through 15 levels of lavishly detailed platform adventure. For the most part, the main challenge was dodging the corporate paraphernalia spewing from the hovering, malevolent smartphone. Occasionally, however, in true *Jumanji* style, an ominous rhyming couplet would herald the arrival of a particular menace, which you would have to defeat before proceeding – the Key Stakeholders were especially difficult to survive, while the encounter with the Chief Risk Officer was truly something to dread. Of course, it all worked out okay in the end – the mother got her baby back, dashed the phone against the rocks of a waterfall, and returned to the deep, chaotic bliss of the forest. It was, without doubt, a feelgood experience. Still, in watching a train full of commuters play this game, primate brows furrowed in an attempt to escape the pinstripe crush around them, one couldn't help but feel brushed by a deep wave of primal sadness.

VERDICT

In a way we're all just apes, flailing in despair at the constant, maddening surfeit of information pouring from our phones each day. And while the fact that *Reverse Jumanji* was itself a smartphone app was something of a bitter irony, its heart was very much in the right place.

SCORE 00567328
TIME 05:54

"IN TRUE *JUMANJI* STYLE, AN OMINOUS RHYMING COUPLET WOULD HERALD THE ARRIVAL OF A PARTICULAR MENACE, WHICH YOU WOULD HAVE TO DEFEAT BEFORE PROCEEDING."

97 POCKET DIOGENES

Whoa look at those!

Pocket Diogenes has accessed your Facebook contacts

VIRTUAL PET BASED ON THE FAMED CYNIC OF ANCIENT GREECE, WHO SPENDS MOST OF HIS TIME EITHER WANKING OR INSULTING YOUR FRIENDS AND FAMILY.

YEAR
Forthcoming

GENRE
Cynic Philosophy / Virtual Pet

DEVELOPER
Digital Beastmasters

FORMAT
Smart watches

While the virtual pet is by no means a new concept for the games industry, it's a genre that hasn't really evolved much over the years. From 1983's *Home Olm*, a simulation of a blind cave salamander for home computers, to the omnipresent handheld *Dog Egg* of the mid-1990s, there was very little innovation in the medium. Even in the twenty-first century, virtual pets like *Eagle in Your Clothes* and *WaspFriend* pretty much stuck to the same formula of roaming listlessly round a virtual prison, occasionally begging for digital nourishment. Now however, with the news that *Pocket Diogenes* is finally set for launch on smart watches (pending the resolution of a few trifling legal questions), all that is set to change. Of course, developer Digital Beastmasters had already dipped their toe in the genre in their 2013 smartphone release *My Untrustworthy Chimp*. This dark piece of software replicated the white-knuckle terror of chimp ownership with a charming little primate that could wander sweetly across a user's phone screen for years, before going berserk and ripping apart all their personal data in a frenzy of bared fangs and simian muscle. Although less brutal, their next project plays with similar themes, but using the philosopher Diogenes as its subject. Diogenes was possibly history's most lovable arsehole. Sleeping in a barrel in the marketplace of ancient Athens, he was renowned for saying what he liked, scoffing at social conventions, and carrying out bodily functions wherever he fancied doing so. He'll take the same approach to living in your watch. *Pocket Diogenes* will have incredible AI, capable of responding to voice requests with a personality incorporating the wisdom of his ancient namesake. But he'll also have access to your phone book, your BookFace contacts, and your bank details. And while the real Diogenes made a virtue of poverty, early indications show that this one will have few qualms about spending your money. He probably won't mind sending inappropriate social media comments to your mates, either. And with a simulated – if casual – awareness of his own mortality, he'll definitely be a pet for life, rather than just for Christmas.

VERDICT

Access to the wisdom of the ancients, at the price of a leering old man living in your watch – a dark bargain, if ever there was one.

"A PET FOR LIFE, RATHER THAN JUST FOR CHRISTMAS."

98 CAR SLEUTH

Elementary my dear driver! It is in fact the next left where the bloodied body was found!

VOICE-CONTROLLED MYSTERY GAME DISGUISED AS A SATNAV APP, WHICH SLOWLY STOPS GIVING YOU DIRECTIONS AND BEGINS CAJOLING YOU INTO SOLVING A MURDER.

YEAR
Forthcoming

GENRE
Mystery / Navigation

DEVELOPER
Strange Directions Software

FORMAT
Satnav

On paper, the forthcoming *Car Sleuth* looks like a smashing concept. Bought for you as a gift by a mischievous friend, it would present itself as a top of the range satnav app, promising to 'unlock the mysteries of the road' with voice work provided by a stable of A-list actors. And for several months, this is exactly what it would do – give you precise and useful driving directions, with occasional vocal flourishes from its stellar cast. But then, at some point when you least expected it, it would strike. "At the next junction, turn right," it might say, before pausing ominously and adding "...unless of course, you want to know what happened to poor Tammy Trifle, in which case you should turn left." Being an inquisitive and adventurous person, you would of course turn left, at which point the app would begin layering the story of an unfolding mystery over the directions to your destination. The type of adventure would be selected based on context – urban fantasy for central London, neo-noir for the inner city, and *Midsomer Murders*-type shit for the countryside. There would be pretend chases, other narrators butting in with twists, and a crime that seemed insoluble, but which would unravel into a satisfying denouement as you pulled into your destination. Again, all sounds great on paper, right? But consider it in practice. You're haring around a godforsaken tangle of rural lanes, kids hollering in the back seat, as your cousin's wedding starts three miles away. You glance frantically at your watch, but Diogenes is just sitting on screen with his balls out, in no mood to help. Then your satnav interjects with "carry straight on at the next roundabout" in the voice of Tom Hardy, and you sigh in relief. But then, as you accelerate in line with the arrows on screen, Jeremy Irons pipes up with "...of course, that's what he *wants* you to think. I think you should turn right." You grimace in sudden rage; this is no time for a mystery. "WHERE'S THE FUCKING CHURCH, IRONS?" you roar, and smack your hand on the wheel, but it's no use. The satnav unit just chuckles darkly, saying "I'm sure you'd love to know. Nevertheless..." but whatever it says next is lost, as it does so from the base of a roadside hedge, where it lies with a cracked screen.

VERDICT

A splendid concept with the potential to backfire horribly, we foresee huge initial sales for *Car Sleuth* before a record number of binnings as real life emerges as the villain of the piece.

"YOU'RE HARING AROUND A GODFORSAKEN TANGLE OF RURAL LANES, KIDS HOLLERING IN THE BACK SEAT, AS YOUR COUSIN'S WEDDING STARTS THREE MILES AWAY."

99

THE GREATEST GATSBY

MYSTERIOUS 1920S MILLIONAIRES ENGAGE IN SAVAGE ARENA COMBAT, UNDER THE PITILESS GAZE OF A STEEL DEBUTANTE.

YEAR
Fothcoming

GENRE
1920s American Decadence / One-on-One Fighter

DEVELOPER
Green Light Interactive

FORMAT
Nintendo Switch

When it is released at the end of the year, this one-on-one fighter for the Nintendo Switch looks like it could sweep the board and set a new benchmark for one-on-one fighting games. From the demo footage released so far, it seems to have left the rest of the genre in the dust, at least in terms of scope. Set in the cosmic inferno of the end of time, it tells the story of D41SY, a godlike artificial intelligence with a penchant for 20th century history, who has decided to curb her epochal boredom by holding a grand gladiatorial tournament for long-dead millionaires. "Can't repeat the past?" the narrator scoffs, as the game's opening credits fade in over a blasted starscape, "why, of course you can!" With these words, a gigantic art deco fortress appears at the heart of a black hole in an explosion of emerald light, and the lavish spectacle begins. This celestial palace is populated with millions of aristocrats transported from countless cultures and eras, all dressed in spotless finery, and with access to infinite champagne and caviar. They are there to indulge in the party to end all parties, and to act as spectators for D41SY's magnificent show. Among them are the game's playable characters: sixteen socially elite champions resurrected from Earth's 1920s, who are there to duel for the ultimate prize – a place as the almighty consort of D41SY herself when she reboots the universe. The game won't just chronicle their actions in the arena before D41SY's throne, either – it'll follow them in between bouts as they feud, reconcile and even find romance with each other. To balance this level of dynamic RPG structure with the crude knockout mechanics of a tournament fighter is unheard of, but from what we've seen so far, it looks like *The Greatest Gatsby* is going to pull it off.

Fun Fact: While cartridges for the Switch are famously coated in an unbearably bitter substance to prevent their ingestion by children or very hungry fools, *The Greatest Gatsby* is to be an exception. In what may turn out to be a very unfortunate move to grab headlines, its cartridge will taste very sightly of champagne and money.

VERDICT

If nothing else, *TGG* deserves respect for the ending of its E3 debut trailer. "So we beat on" intoned the narrator, over footage of dazzling fist fights, "boats against the current, borne forward ceaselessly into the future… to batter each other."

"A GODLIKE ARTIFICIAL INTELLIGENCE WITH A PENCHANT FOR TWENTIETH CENTURY HISTORY."

100 'TIL BLUTO DO US PART

EXPERIENCE VIGNETTES OF A COUPLE'S LIFE TOGETHER, BUT THE MEMORIES ARE CONSTANTLY INVADED BY BLUTO FROM POPEYE

YEAR
Fothcoming

GENRE
Bluto / Interactive Movie

DEVELOPER
Coole Swan Games

FORMAT
Unknown

The smell of honeysuckle drifts on the evening breeze, tangled with the dusky warbling of skylarks, as the couple stroll through the garden together. Putting a staying hand on his beloved's shoulder, the young man says he has something to show her. As she turns, the wetness of her eyes betrays the fact she has guessed what comes next. He sees it as he meets her gaze, and can't hide a grin. She laughs in delight, and he sinks to one knee, fumbling for a small hinged box. He opens it, she peers down at its padded interior, and her smile collapses in horror. Inside, as clear as day, is a bright enamel pin badge bearing the grimacing likeness of Bluto, Popeye's ruffian nemesis. Before she can form words, there is a burly rustling in the bushes behind them, followed by an incomprehensible, bear-like growl, and a blurry cartoon figure advances with a self-hating swagger. This is the content of the demo for *'Til Bluto Do Us Part*, a VR title slated for release next year, and it's hard to know how to interpret it. From rare interviews with the game's reclusive developer, it seems it will take the form of a sort of interactive film, in which various scenes from a couple's long life together have been filmed using an omnidirectional camera, so players can view them from any angle. But there is a grim twist: at the emotional climax of every scene, whether joyful or poignant, the action is invaded and ruined by the thuggish, animated form of Bluto. He doesn't hurt anyone, nor does he threaten to – but he kills the moment every time. He can't be stopped, nor can the scene's participants be warned of his arrival. Indeed, every time he appears, it is as if they are surprised. As a player you are just a silent observer, drawing whatever beauty you can from these scenes before the inevitable unfolds. Is this a reflection on the developer's own experience of love? Is it a comment on the looming inevitability of death, and the importance of living in the moment in a world of chaos and suffering? Or is it just a game about what an arsehole Bluto is? It's probably that last one, to be honest. The guy was a complete dick to Popeye, after all.

VERDICT

Sometimes in this life, despite everything leading you to expect a happy ending, all you get is Bluto. But if you can learn to laugh at Bluto himself, there's nothing left to fear.

"THE ACTION IS INVADED AND RUINED BY THE THUGGISH, ANIMATED FORM OF BLUTO."

EPILOGUE
FUTURE TRENDS IN GAMING

Over the last fifty years, no area of human technology has advanced as quickly as computer science, and games have always ridden on the crest of that wave, like a cool dude on a surfboard made of loads of little ones and zeroes. As we hurtle into a future where digital technology is only going to get more and more incomprehensibly powerful, you can bet that games developers will be there, using every new development to advance their art. While it's near impossible to say what wonders may tumble from the great neon arse of the future, we can certainly have a go, plus it seems a nice way to finish off the book – so let's have it:

REAL CONSEQUENCES

We've all heard the cliche in straight-to-video cyberthrillers from the 80s: when you die in the game, YOU DIE IN REAL LIFE. But with technology reportedly being tested in the world of illegal underground e-sports, this could soon be a reality. Imagine an FPS deathmatch where the losing player's heart is stopped for a full minute, before a medical team rushes onstage with defibrillators, and you're imagining one hell of a dystopian hypersport.

GAMES AS A JOB

While we've already seen the advent of people playing games for a living, such as the gold farmers who make their crust from grinding monsters in MMOs, increasing levels of automation replacing jobs, plus the growing economic importance of the games sector, may mean that a significant slice of the population will end up playing games as a career. Let's just hope they don't end up playing any of the shitter games in this collection.

LIVING IN GAMES

Why stop at playing games as a day job, however? As demonstrated by the intriguing case of *Realms of Fightinge*, it may one day be possible for people to live inside them entirely. With a team of coders currently working round the clock to reverse engineer the infamous 'Install Wizard' software that uploaded Colin Colinson into *RoF*, that day may come sooner than we think.

NO BARRIERS TO ENTRY

With the growth of the indie studio scene, and the creation of increasingly user-friendly development tools, it's becoming easier and easier for anyone who's interested to make their own games. Will children end up making their own bizarre triple-A creations that adults will completely fail to understand due to the baffling logic involved? Will a dog make a game this century? We fucking hope so.

EVEN BETTER AI

Gamers currently rely on multiplayer functionality to experience the thrill of fighting against or beside characters that can think for themselves, but it won't be long before software is up to the task. We're beginning to see this already – in last year's *Phantom Recon with Brian Blessed*, renowned as the hardest military stealth experience ever made, the game's titular squadmate was so deafeningly jovial that many players could swear they were playing alongside the man himself.

GAMIFICATION OF REAL LIFE

Given the sheer amount of collective mental energy that goes into the analysis of virtual card games, the writing of obscure erotic mods for epic RPGs, and the creation of Wikipedia entries for 1990s platform game characters, it's only a matter of time before someone finds a way to harness this energy for a real world project. If the dedication that went into the writing and critique of *Ricky Feathers* fanfiction were diverted into the space program, we'd be living on Mars within ten years. Dressed as owls.

DRONES

The increasing ubiquity of tiny robotic flying machines controlled with a joystick from a remote location is practically begging for the sort of horrendous technosocial changes that make *Jurassic Park* look like a sound risk proposition. Give it twenty years, and wars will definitely be fought by proxy, and by generals with screen names like *Deathlass420xXx* and *BiscuitKing69*.

STREAMING

If there's one thing the last five years have taught us, it's that people love watching other people playing games almost as much as – if not more than – playing games themselves. At this point, the next logical step is for people to begin watching streams of other people watching streams, or for characters in games to begin watching broadcasts of everyday human activity. Yeah, that.

GAMES WITH NO HARDWARE

While the advent of VR technology, motion sensor peripherals and the like has led to something of a renaissance in the manufacture and sale of games-related hardware, there will likely come a point where games can be experienced with nothing more than the human brain itself. Although the prospect of starting a game of *Jimmy Bumshow* just by thinking about it presents, perhaps more than any other item on this list, a truly nightmarish vision of things to come.

GROND

One thing that continues to mystify commentators on the games industry is how, more than 60 years after its debut in print and 15 years after it first appeared on the silver screen, we are yet to see a game entirely focused on the character of Grond, the blazing, wolf-headed battering ram from *The Lord of the Rings: The Return of the King*. A nuanced character full of wolf-headed charm and the honest desire to smash gates asunder, it seems Grond would be the perfect protagonist across any genre from romance to legal procedural. But alas, the industry still refuses to cotton on to this basic truth. Grond. Grond. GROND!